To

LOSS & RESTORATION

with best wishes

Fred Flatow

LOSS &
RESTORATION
Stories
from
Three Continents

by
Fred Flatow

Brixton Publisher

Brixton Publisher

9913 Brixton Lane

Bethesda, MD 20817

Designed and produced by The Magazine Group

Library of Congress Catalog Card Number 98-92655

ISBN: 0-9663933-0-9

I DEDICATE THIS BOOK TO the memory of my murdered friends and family, and to all those unknowns, German and Chilean, Jewish and not Jewish, who more than half a century ago made it possible for me to survive when so many others died.

Preface

I WROTE THIS ACCOUNT IN RESPONSE TO QUESTIONS FROM MY CHILDREN and grandchildren about our lives before we came to the United States. Their interest was centered particularly on events in Germany and what it was like to grow up under the Nazi regime before the Holocaust had begun. They also wanted to know what life had been like in our exile country, Chile, and how it happened that we finally came to the United States.

There were other reasons to record my life. There are many books, articles and reports by Holocaust survivors who survived the camps or escaped deportation and survived in Germany itself. Their courage, their suffering and the painful process of readjustment once they were freed from hell provide a unique testimonial to the human spirit. This account tells a different story. It deals with what it was like for a child to grow up in Germany after 1933, emigrate to a foreign country before the final catastrophe and leave friends and family behind who were later all brutally exterminated. What was it like to learn the language and ways of a new country? To adjust to the emotional impact and economic pressures occasioned by immigration? To construct a new life from the debris of the Nazi terror? In describing my case and that of my family, I hope to provide answers to some of these questions.

I think it is important that the historical record of the Nazi rise to power and the impact of the anti-Semitic policies be recorded to the fullest possible extent. The organized attacks on German Jews started with boycotts of Jewish businesses, continued with the exclusion of Jews from Germany's economic and cultural life, produced the first large-scale violence during the infamous Crystal Night and proceeded to the industrialized murder that took place in the extermination camps. Too few Jews saw the full extent of the danger; too few left in time. My family got out at the last possible minute. Consequently, I am not a survivor in the sense that the word is usually interpreted, that is, a survivor of the Holocaust. But I was a victim of the Nazi rise to power nevertheless, and I am a different kind of survivor, as were my parents and my brother.

Due to these considerations, I decided not only to write about Germany, but extend the story to the rebuilding of my life which spanned two additional continents, two additional countries, two more languages and two very different cultures.

All the events described in this account are "true" in the large sense. But memory being what it is, I may remember some of the events in ways different from the "objective" facts, particularly in the first section where I recount my early childhood. Yet, I have a strong sense of what it was like to grow up in my native city, Königsberg, which was a rabid nest of anti-Semitism. What I experienced there left a deep impression on me—too deep for me to ever forget. My memories of the few months I lived in Hamburg just before leaving Germany are equally strong, and surviving letters have been used to supplement what I have been able to recall. My memories from Chile are more precise because I was older then. Even so, I found that some of my memories were distorted and that I had forgotten certain happenings. Fortunately, I kept a diary for five years from 1942 to 1947, which I have used to correct the tricks that memory plays and to help me recall once forgotten events.

I want to thank my wife, Ursel, also known as Sue, for patiently reading my manuscript and making suggestions on how to improve it as it progressed through a series of drafts. I am grateful to my friend Lore Hepner in far-off Santiago, Chile, for her ideas and comments. I am also grateful to Dr. Stefanie Schüler-Springorum and Dr. Irmtrud Wojak for providing historical background regarding the Jewish communities in Königsberg and Santiago respectively. Dr. Diane Spielmann of the Leo Baeck Institute also provided valuable material related to the Jewish community in Königsberg. Tim Wells read the nearly completed manuscript, made suggestions on how to organize it to make it more readable and edited the final draft. Without them I could not have written this account.

Deutschland, Deutschland...

I AM ALIVE TODAY NOT BECAUSE MY PARENTS PLANNED AN ESCAPE FROM threatening disaster—to the contrary, they were confident that the Nazi threats would disappear and that we would be able to continue our lives as German citizens, much as we had done in the years before the arrival of the Nazi menace. But it was not to be. I am alive today because an event designed to destroy us turned into the opposite and saved our lives. We were among the lucky few to leave Germany after all hope for escape had vanished.

In the Beginning
The July 1928 bulletin of the Jewish Community in Königsberg, the *Gemein-deblatt*, reported the birth of a son to the merchant Erich Flatow on May 16. The mother's name, Malwine, called Pina ("Peena") by everybody, was omitted in the announcement. She was not considered important. The other announce-ments in the bulletin were similar: only the fathers were mentioned. The happy parents gave their new baby three names: Siegfried Friedel Ernst. The name Ernst because the name of my mother's mother, a grandmother I never knew, had been Ernestine. She had been dead for many years at the time I was born. The other two names need an explanation.

Four days before my birth, my father's only sister had died of tuberculosis at the age of forty-one. While my mother was in the hospital giving birth, he was at the cemetery burying his sister. She was called Frieda—Friedel for short—and my father wanted to memorialize her name. My arrival gave him the opportunity he sought. He wanted me to be called Friedel. Although my father insisted, my mother could not see her son going through life being called Friedel because it was an ambiguous, somewhat effeminate, unisex name. They reached a compromise: Friedel would be my second name, but my first name would be Siegfried, the name of the legendary hero of the Germanic Nibelungen saga. One way for German Jews to show how patriotic they were was to name their children after the legendary Ger-man heroes. As a result, many Jewish children bore the names of heroes of the peo-ple who took away their jobs, robbed them of their wealth, pushed them into exile, and murdered those unable to leave. But soon I acquired a nickname, "Schieps" (like in sheep's), and for the next twelve or thirteen years I was known by that name.

My mother was already forty-two years old when I was born, and there were no more children. She had married late, at the age of thirty-eight. Her first child, my older brother Manfred, was born in 1925, a year after her marriage.

The first apartment I remember overlooked the city's main street, two flights up from the street. There were two maids: one to cook and clean, the other a nursemaid named *Fräulein* Martha. It was a large apartment, and I had my own room. I slept in a white metal crib with high railings that had large black smudges next to my head. The smudges were there because one day when I was three years old, I got hold of a box of matches and set the bed on fire. One of the maids smelled the smoke and extinguished the flames.

Often my father came in to sleep his siesta on the sofa opposite my crib. When this happened, his loud snores kept me awake. The room was next to the dining room, and at times when I was supposed to sleep, I could hear the nursemaid as she tried to feed my brother, urging him to swallow his lunch instead of keeping it in his mouth in a pouch he formed with his cheeks. My brother often woke up from his nap with his food still in that pouch and at those times he would be loudly scolded.

Our apartment was located on *Vorstädtische Langgasse*, which translates to "Suburban Long Alley"—but the street was neither long nor was it in the suburbs. In earlier times its two lanes were used only by horse drawn carts, but now both carts and automobiles passed beneath our apartment windows. Soon the horse carts and the cars had to share the busy street with Nazi Storm Troopers marching along singing their boisterous, hate-filled songs. Streetcars ran along the middle of the street. Sometimes, especially in winter, horses would fall and die while drawing their loaded carts. Then, all traffic came to a standstill. The street led from the main railroad station at one end to the ancient castle in the center of town. On its way it crossed two of the seven bridges spanning the river Pregel. For many years a famous mathematical question had been asked about these bridges. The question was whether a path could be found that crossed all seven bridges once and only once. In the 18th century a mathematician named Leonhard Euler demonstrated that it could not be done.

The castle was the pride and symbol of Königsberg. Prussian kings had built it beginning in the 15th century and a tower was added one-hundred years later. When I visited the castle, I had to take off my shoes and put on slippers. The floors had been polished to such a high gloss that I could see my reflection in them. Nearby, on an island formed by two branches of the river, stood the almost equally ancient *Dom*, the cathedral. A memorial to the philosopher Immanuel Kant, a native of the city, was built into one of its outer walls. When I was eight, I was taken to the old philosopher's house, which had been converted into a museum. The house stood near the castle in an ancient, narrow street lined with similar 18th century houses. Kant was small and his house was small: two or three rooms, furnished with a desk, a table and bookcases. To philosophize did not require much space.

The home of another famous native of the city who was still living at the time was off limits. This was the artist Käthe Kollwitz. The Nazi authorities did not like her art because the drawings and woodcuts for which she was famous depicted poor and suffering people at a time when the government wanted to show only the opposite: a Germany that was prosperous, satisfied, healthy and happy.

A Little History: The City and Its Jewish Community

I always wanted to know when it was that Jews had first settled in my hometown and where they had come from. I asked myself whether it was possible to trace the history of my ancestors, even if there were no records after the destruction of the city in World War II. I did find at least a few of the answers.

Königsberg[1] was the capital of East Prussia, a province of Germany located in the northeastern corner of the country. As a result of the Great War of 1914, it was separated from the rest of the country by the "Polish Corridor," a stretch of land that had belonged to Germany before the war but was now part of Poland.

In 1255 German knights founded Königsberg as a fortress from which they subjugated local tribes and appropriated their lands. Although the knights allowed two Jewish physicians to settle in the city in 1538 and 1541 respectively, Jews were not permitted to take up permanent residence until the 18th century. Jewish merchants, mostly from Poland, could trade in the city and live there temporarily for that purpose, but Jews who settled in the city in violation of the residence prohibition were expelled.

In spite of the expulsions, Jews from neighboring countries continued to drift to Königsberg. By the middle of the 17th century, the residence restrictions had been eased for a few well-to-do Jews. The ruling dukes profited from this arrangement because they made the wealthy Jews pay heavy fees and taxes for every privilege granted to them. Poor Jewish traders, unable to pay the required fees, were still excluded. In 1680 permission was granted to the Jews living in Königsberg to open a prayer room. But they could not bury their dead within the confines of the city. Deceased Jews had to be transported to Poland for burial— a distance of about thirty miles. It was not until 1704 that a Jewish cemetery was

---

[1] Stefanie Schüler-Springorum, "Jüdisch-Bürgerliches Leben in Königsberg/Pr. 1880–1945," M.A. Thesis for the University of Göttingen (1987); "Die jüdische Minderheit in Königsberg/Pr. 1871–1945," doctoral dissertation with the same title for the Fakultät für Geschichtswissenschaft der Ruhr-Universität Bochum; and a book based on the doctoral dissertation, Vandenhoeck & Ruprecht, 1996. I am also grateful for her personal communications on the subject.

established and a burial society, *Chevra Kadisha,* was founded. The beginning of Königsberg's Jewish community is commonly dated to that event. In 1712 there were 36 Jewish families in Königsberg. The men were craftsmen and small traders. In many cases wives augmented the family income by running kitchens and guest houses for Jewish travelers. By 1745 the Jewish community was large enough to employ a rabbi, a ritual slaughterer, a teacher and a *shammes* (sexton). In the same year, a Jewish hospital was also founded. Finally, in 1756, permission was granted for the establishment of a synagogue.

During the 18th century, a few wealthy Jewish families began to associate with the enlightened circles of non-Jewish society in Königsberg. As early as the second half of that century, there were conflicts between these "enlightened" Jews who spoke German and the traditional orthodox Jews who frequently spoke Yiddish. Reform-minded Jews started to provide their children with "worldly" education, and their sons went to the university. In 1847 Jewish reformers rented a hall for religious services that were conducted in German and held on Sundays. Twenty years later the reform was extended to high holiday services, which included an organ, a choir, a sermon in German and a special prayer book. Traditionalists, primarily comprised of residents from the surrounding non-German regions, fought liberalization. Although the reform movement gained strength, it lost many of its members to Christian conversions, with most of them becoming Protestants. Between 1800 and 1846, 245 Jews converted. Initially it was primarily "upper class" Jews who converted, but in 1835, poor Jews began to convert in hope of improving their lot. They were joined by newcomers from Russia who hoped to gain residency and entree into the upper classes.

On the 11th of March, 1812, an edict granted citizenship to the Jewish residents of East Prussia that guaranteed the right of Jewish residence in Königsberg. One of the Jews who acquired his citizenship on that day was my great-great grandfather on my father's side, Leib Lewin ben Simon, that is, Leib Lewin, the son of Simon. Before emancipation, Jews did not have family names. They were known by their first names and as the son or daughter of the man who was their father. This changed when the Prussian authorities required that all emancipated Jews give themselves family names. They could choose their own names. If they did not, the authorities picked one for them. Some Jews simply took the name of their place of origin. That is how my family name was acquired. Flatow was a village in West Prussia. Others took their trade as their name, for example, Goldschmidt (goldsmith). At the time of his emancipation, my great-great grandfather became Leo Lewin Zeimann. I do not know the origin of that name. According to family lore, it is a unique name and all people in the world called Zeimann are related.

After the 1812 edict, the Jewish community in Königsberg prospered. It was estimated that in 1800 more than ninety percent of the Jewish population was poor, but by 1864 the percentage of the poor had become negligible. Jews were working in all professions except government. There were seventeen Jewish physicians in the city. Although excluded from government employment, Jews were members of the City Council.

Jews living in the surrounding provinces were attracted to East Prussia's capital city by the greater social, economic and educational opportunities available there. There was also a much larger Jewish community in the city—approximately 3,000 by the middle of the 19th century. Both my paternal and maternal ancestors came to Königsberg between 1860 and 1880 from West Prussia. Other Jews came from Poland and Lithuania.

The Jewish community of Königsberg always remained small. In 1700, there were fifty Jews out of a total population of 40,600. The high point was reached in 1880, when there were 5,324 Jews out of a population of approximately 141,000. When I was born in 1928, the number had declined to 3,200. By May of 1939, four months before the outbreak of World War II, only 1,586 Jews remained. After the deportations by the Nazis, the Jewish community officially ceased to exist in 1943. When the war ended in 1945 only a handful of Jews remained: half-Jews and some who lived in mixed marriages.

The First School Year: German Public School

In April of 1934, when I was almost six, I began to go to school. It was exciting. I had been in kindergarten, but this was different. I looked forward to my first day of school, but I was also a little nervous. In a corner of my room stood the customary *Schultüte,* a cone shaped cardboard container filled to the brim with candy, which all first-graders were given on their first school day. That morning my mother and I walked from our house to the school a few blocks away. I carried the *Schultüte* and a satchel with a notebook and some pencils, which I soon used for my first efforts at writing. It was a public school for boys only; girls had their own school. There were perhaps thirty boys carrying the same things I did. We entered a classroom where our teacher, a woman, welcomed us. My mother left with the other mothers, and I was left to face what was to come by myself. Initially, all went well, but after only a few weeks it was clear to me that I was different. I was an outsider. This was 1934, a year after Hitler had come to power, and his influence was making itself felt even among six-year-olds. Every day classes started with the Hitler salute and the whole class shouted "*Heil* Hitler!" This was the Nazi version of the Pledge of Allegiance. I did not participate in this ritual, and the teacher did not expect me to. I was the only exception. There were no other Jewish boys in the class. Many of the boys were already members of Nazi youth organizations, and some wore swastika insignias on their shirts and jackets. Soon they started to direct their hostility at the Jew in their class. Young as they were, they already knew that Jews were their enemy. They had been taught that we were bent on destroying their beloved fatherland. They called me names, and would taunt me by sneering *Jude*, Jew, which in their opinion was an insult. Sometimes during class breaks when we were in the school yard, they would hit me and grab the things that I was carrying. The teachers supervising the yard did not intervene to protect me. Either they were Nazis themselves, or they were afraid to intervene on behalf of a Jewish child. Not all of the children behaved like that. The bullies who taunted and attacked me were always the same. There was one boy sitting next to me in class who never participated in these attacks. He had freckles and was quiet, and I sensed that he had some sympathy for what was happening to me. I had no other friends and would have liked to have him as a friend. But that was impossible. No "Aryan" child could have a Jewish friend. I sometimes wondered why he was so different. Was he just passive? Did he come from a home that had not fallen under the Nazi influence?

I was afraid of the children, of the school and of the teacher. I was not a good student. I neglected my homework. When the teacher asked for it, I lied and said that my mother had told me not to do it. More than once Mother was called to school to discuss my behavior. She was angry with me and scolded me, but my behavior did not change. I could not improve in that fearful environment.

I only lasted one year. Beginning with the second grade, I was enrolled in a new Jewish school that had been founded to meet the needs of children who could not stay in the public schools—children who had experienced what I had experienced, or worse. The school was located in the New Synagogue, and it had been founded by the liberal segment of the Jewish community.

The Synagogue

We were members of the liberal sector of the Jewish community and attended religious services in the New Synagogue. The building, with its 160 foot high dome visible from many parts of the city, had been inaugurated in 1896. Its Moorish style was similar to synagogues built in other German cities around the same time. It was not the only synagogue in town, but it was by far the largest. It stood as a symbol of a proud and prosperous Jewish community with members secure in their role as citizens of their town and country. Conservative Jews belonged to the Old Synagogue located on a street parallel to the grounds of the factory at which my parents earned their living. The street was appropriately called *Synagogenstrasse*, later changed to *Seilerstrasse* in the 1930s. In addition, there were two tiny ultra-orthodox prayer rooms, *shuls,* one in an alley right around the corner from our apartment, the other a short distance away. There was little contact between the three traditional congregations and the liberals, and what contact there was, was usually antagonistic. The conflict between tradition and reform, between the old and the new, had lasted more than two centuries and showed no signs of abating. Yet to state it in these terms, old and new, is too simplistic. Traditionalists themselves were split into several factions, and in Königsberg it required three, and at times four, synagogues to accommodate all the differences in their religious beliefs and practices. The same was true for the reformers. In Königsberg there was only one liberal synagogue, but in other parts of the country, such as Berlin, there were several, and they were needed to accommodate a similar variety of liberal beliefs and practices. As is true even now in America, Israel and many other parts of the world, it was impossible to accommodate all factions under one roof. Compromise and tolerance for one another were difficult to achieve.

Some Friday evenings and on many of the holidays, I went to the synagogue with my father. On these occasions he wore a black top hat, as did most other men who came to services. I thought the hat made my father look dignified. But it also invited the undesired attention of anti-Semitic Germans who celebrated different holidays, and whose day of rest was not the Sabbath, but Sunday. When my father wore his top hat, we drew stares and unfriendly remarks. I felt secure only after we were inside the synagogue. As the political situation grew worse, the synagogue issued a recommendation for men to come to services with their top hats wrapped up and to put their hats on only after they were inside the building. It took us about twenty minutes to walk to the synagogue. It was a pleasant walk and rarely did we use the streetcar, even though it had a stop right in front, and we never went by car. We had once owned a car, driven by a chauffeur who was an employee of the factory, but it had been sold. Few people had cars, none of our family or friends owned one. The synagogue had no parking facilities.

I was awed by this building. Its facade with its three entrance portals topped by the towering cupola gave me a feeling of solidity, of something that would last forever. The inside of the building was as beautiful as it was impressive on the outside. The main sanctuary ended in a multilevel altar, the *bima*. On its highest level there was a closet-like enclosure hidden from view by a richly decorated curtain. This was the repository of the *Torah* scrolls, the holy scrolls inscribed in Hebrew with the five books of Moses, handwritten on parchment by specially trained scribes. Wealthy members considered it an honor to commission the writing of a scroll and to donate it to the synagogue. There were about two dozen of them, each dressed in a velvet cover like a skirt and decorated with heavy silver ornaments. I was proud that my family had donated one of these scrolls. One or two were taken out each Saturday and on holidays for the chanting of portions of the Torah, either by the cantor or a male member of the congregation. The level below the curtain was reserved for the cantor. When the *Torah* was to be read, actually chanted, it would be brought from the higher level and put down on a special table to be unrolled for the reading. Opening the curtain of the depository, carrying the *Torah* and saying the blessing over it were all considered honors handed out during each service to deserving members of the congregation. Also on this level was a pulpit from which the rabbi delivered his sermons. High above the *bima* was the organ whose large pipes soared heavenward like outstretched fingers reaching for God. This was the domain of the organist, a Christian whose name was Jacobus. A choir sat on either side of the organ, with men on one side and women on the other, and performed at all services. The organ and the choir had always caused conflict with the more orthodox congregations that regarded them as an abomination. The children were welcome to watch the organist as he practiced, and many were the times when I climbed the stairs to do so. Sometimes the friendly Jacobus allowed me to play the organ. On one occasion while the organist was practicing, Nazi Storm Troopers came up and terrorized Jacobus and the children watching him. On this occasion nothing happened beyond the shouting and the threats. No damage was done, nobody was hurt. After a while the Nazis had enough of their fun and left. The frightened children left a little while later.

The *bima* was framed by a high arch, soaring above the tall organ pipes, encircling them. The liberal label not withstanding, women were segregated in a second story gallery surrounding the main floor sanctuary, just as demanded by more orthodox Jewish custom. The gallery seated 600 women, while the main floor accommodated 710 men. My father owned a permanent seat on the right side of the synagogue close to the front. My mother's seat was on the left so that they could look at each other during services. It also gave her a chance to make sure I behaved when I was seated next to my father.

One morning in October 1935, I was awakened by my favorite cousin Lola, the daughter of my father's sister, Friedel, who was twelve years older than me. She told me that my grandmother (the mother of my father and my only surviving grandparent) had died the previous evening. I accepted this information as a matter of fact and experienced no sense of loss. Later in the day I heard a conversation between my parents and Lola. My parents did not want me to attend the funeral. I was too young, they said. But I wanted to go. Lola took my side and argued that I was grown and that it was necessary that I experience not only life but death as well. Lola won. My parents relented. The next day we left in a car to go to the cemetery. I was seated next to Lola, who held my hand. We got to the cemetery, entered a small building next to the entrance where the casket stood surrounded by flowers. I sat a little to the back where I could look at my parents as well as the rabbi. He lead a brief ceremony, saying a few words to my father and reciting the required prayers. Then the casket was carried out to the grave where my grandfather had been buried fifteen years earlier. We all walked behind the casket, with my parents going first. The casket was lowered into the open grave and my father recited the traditional prayer over the dead, the *Kaddish*. At the end he took a small shovel and threw some earth into the grave. The sand falling on the casket produced an eerie hollow sound and at that moment my father broke down and cried. I had never seen him cry before, and I never saw him do so again. It was only then that I shared his sense of loss.

The Friday evening of that same week I accompanied my father to the synagogue. He wore a black band around his left elbow, and a black band around his top hat. This time he did not enter the main sanctuary with me but stayed behind in the small chapel located at the entrance of the sanctuary. He was not allowed to attend the service until after the traditional hymn welcoming the Sabbath as a bride had been sung by the congregation. When that hymn finished, I turned around and saw my father as he was led into the synagogue by the sexton. The rabbi met him halfway down the sanctuary and spoke some comforting words. My father looked sad and I remembered the scene at the grave site when he had cried.

I always loved the organ and chorus that accompanied all the services. For me the melodies were one of the reasons I liked to attend services. I was not alone in that. The synagogue was famous for the music that had been composed earlier in the century by its cantor, Edward Birnbaum. This religious music had such an emotional impact that it came to influence the liturgy not only in many synagogues, but even in some Protestant churches. It always gave me a thrill when the cantor, Rudolf Pik, who had been an opera singer before he became a cantor, sang the beautiful melodies. I remember them to this day. But I feared the rabbi, Reinhold Lewin. He looked so stern. Not once did he invite children up to the *bima* to participate in services except on *Simchat Torah* (Joy of the *Torah*), a holiday when all the scrolls were taken out and carried in a parade around the synagogue. Like all the other children, I participated in the parade every year. I carried a flag. Other children, who were lucky enough to own a miniature *Torah*—printed, not hand-written—would carry it instead of a flag. The parade went around all the seats and was repeated several times. The organ played joyful music, and a lot of noise was made by the children. At the end, the scrolls were returned to the repository and we were given candy—the supreme moment of the whole event.

In 1935 room was made for the classrooms of the new Jewish School. Almost all young children of the Jewish community attended this school whether they were religious or not. Their presence in the public schools had become an impossibility, just as it had been for me. Some older children continued to attend higher level schools, in particular the pre-university *Gymnasium*, because our new school could only accommodate students in the lower grades. My brother was among those who continued at the *Gymnasium*. He claimed that while some of his co-students were anti-Semitic, his teachers were not. But he was also envious of the other students: their security compared to his insecurity, their uniforms and the group spirit from which he was excluded.

Behind the synagogue there was a small yard, where I, together with other children, planted flowers and vegetables during the summer. Each of us was assigned a minuscule plot. I loved that work and spent many happy hours caring for my plants. There was a magnificent plum tree that we raided when the fruit was ripe. At the back of the yard was a fence that gave access to the Jewish orphanage next door. A few years later that fence was destined to play an important role in my life.

The Jewish School

In April 1935 the Jewish School[2] started to operate, thus relieving the intolerable situation many Jewish children had endured in the public schools. There were four classes and eighty-two children, served by two full-time teachers and one teacher who was employed half-time. One-and-a-half years later, the school had

---

[2] A good description (in German) of the Jewish School can be found in "Die Jüdische Schule in Königsberg/Pr." by Franz Kaelter, the school's principal. It is published in the Bulletin of the Leo Baeck Institute, #14, 1961, p. 145.

180 children, six classes and six teachers. I was a student from the very beginning, and now I looked forward to going to school. I no longer felt the fear and insecurity of my year in public school. I was no longer abused for being a Jew. For the first time I had friends. The other children felt the same. Everybody was accepted, nobody beat them or called them names for being Jewish. The teachers were kind and understanding, and fully dedicated to us. They made us feel safe and secure. Of the six teachers, three were men and three were women. To me, they all seemed the same age—old. But pictures I saw later revealed that the male teachers were only in their twenties. One of the female teachers, Kaete Hiller, was a close friend of my mother. Outside the school I called her *Tante*, aunt, the customary way of addressing close family friends.

In this secure environment I was a good student, except in English where I once got a failing grade. I did my homework. I didn't need to lie about it, and my mother was never called to the school due to my bad behavior. I was happy. Much to my surprise, I later found out that I was also a "darling" of the school; liked by teachers and students.

I was nine when the school organized its last excursion by boat to one of the nearby beaches. Both parents and children were welcome. It was the last excursion because from that time forward the boat company refused to rent to the Jewish School. This was the only time I went on such a trip. I looked forward to the excursion and arrived early at the dock where the boat was tied up at the quay. It was a large tug boat named *Siegfried* that at other times helped freighters navigate the river. The day was bright, and the mood of the children was happy. It promised to be a beautiful occasion. During the two hours long voyage, we sat on benches set up on the deck for the occasion. When we arrived at the beach on the Baltic Sea we had it all to ourselves because the school authorities had scouted it out beforehand to ensure that it was solitary. Nobody molested us, nobody taunted us. We swam, enjoyed the sun and the food and played games. In the late afternoon when the sun was about to set, we said good-bye to the beach and boarded the tug to start on our journey home. It had been a great day, and we were happy. Songs filled the air as we were riding home. We did not realize then that this joyful experience would never be repeated.

Occasionally the outside world penetrated the closed little world of Jewish children. One day toward the end of September 1938, I came to class as usual. During the previous days I had heard my parents discuss the possibility that war would break out because of Hitler's threats to invade a region of Czechoslovakia known as the *Sudetenland*. I was worried and so was everybody else in my class. But the teachers said that the matter had been settled, that there would be no war. They said that the leaders of the most important countries in Europe had met in Munich and come to an agreement. We did not understand that this agreement sacrificed Czechoslovakia to Hitler as a form of blackmail to maintain the peace in Europe, and that the country most affected by the agreement, Czechoslovakia, had not been given any voice in the settlement. The teachers expressed gratitude that war had been prevented. They told us that the British prime minister, Neville Chamberlain, had proclaimed that "peace in our time" was a reality. Neither teachers, students nor parents knew that "our time" would only last 11 months.

When we talked about the world outside, we did it ever so carefully. We were all aware of the ever-watchful eye of the *Gestapo*, Germany's dreaded secret police. Some mornings when I arrived at school, or during class breaks, I saw strange men prowling the hallways. They were *Gestapo* agents. Seeing them I sensed danger. So did everybody else.

One day in 1938, a little girl from the school came to lunch at our house. Times had grown harder. Some families no longer had enough to eat. The school principal asked the more prosperous families to invite the children of these poorer families into their homes, and this little girl was assigned to us. When we came home, she sat at our dining table with her hands in her lap and did not eat. She was shy and I could see that she was intimidated by the formal dining room, my mother and the maid who served the food. After a few weeks she relaxed enough to eat a few bites. She ate with us once a week. On the days she came to our house, I walked home with her. I did not like her and thought she was ugly and not too clean. Never having experienced poverty, I did not understand what it meant to be poor and was too young to feel compassion. One day my mother found half-masticated food hidden under the tablecloth where the little girl sat. Mother's sense of propriety was offended and she scolded the girl. I felt guilty in some undefined way, and I was embarrassed by my mother's behavior. That was the last time the girl came to our house for lunch. My mother did not take her back. Perhaps she too had yet to learn the meaning of compassion.

Fear

The Nazi party was active early in Königsberg. The local branch was one of the most viciously anti-Semitic in Germany. Violent incidents started soon after the new *N.S.D.A.P.*[3] *Gauleiter* (regional leader), Erich Koch, was appointed in 1929.

---

[3] National Sozialistische Deutsche Arbeiterpartei: National Socialist German Workers Party.

In 1933, the Nazis murdered a Jew, and arson attempts were made on a synagogue and Jewish businesses that March. Jewish leaders were beaten—sometimes at the Nazi party headquarters. The police were powerless to stop these brutal actions. The president of the police resigned in 1933 to protest his loss of power.[4] These events marked a serious escalation of the latent anti-Semitism that had always been present in the local population, but such violence was not just a quantitative escalation, it was a radical departure from the past.

Among my earliest memories is the May Day parade of 1934, when Hitler's uniformed brownshirts marched down the main street; column after column roared songs that glorified the Nazi party and threatened the destruction of the Jews. I watched from our balcony overlooking the street. Our nursemaid stood next to me and held my hand. I was only five years old. Although the nursemaid was not Jewish, perhaps she was afraid too. At that moment I became aware of a fear that never left me as long as I remained in Germany. I became aware that I was a despised outsider, that I did not belong. I learned what it meant to be a Jew: Jews were enemies of the "real Germans" and we had to be destroyed.

How was I identified as a Jew? How did the boys in the public school know? What instinct told them that I was Jewish? Did I look different? Was my hair darker? Was there something in my face? (Certainly, not my nose, it was quite small.) Was it my name? Did the teacher tell them? If so, how did the teacher know? There were other boys with dark hair. Not all non-Jews were blond. There were other children with "non-Aryan" faces—whatever that was. Later, when I walked to the Jewish school, boys who did not know me, dressed in the uniforms of the Nazi youth organizations, taunted and threw stones at me. How did they know I was Jewish? They appeared long before I reached the synagogue, long before they could know where I was headed. Perhaps there really was a "Jewish look" that people recognized. Not all Jews had that look. Some Jews looked like the blond-haired, blue-eyed Germanic type that was the Nazi ideal, and they were not recognized as Jews. But they were the exceptions. And not all non-Jews looked Aryan: some were mistaken for Jews.

On an official level it was easy enough for the authorities to determine who was Jewish. There were birth and family registrations that stated an individual's religion, and there was a religious tax paid to the government and then distributed to the various religious organizations. Few, if any, could escape the tax. (Even today such a tax continues to be deducted from income in Germany and

---

[4] Schüler-Springorum, op. cit.

distributed to the respective churches.) But how did this translate into identifications in everyday life? Unlike many Jews living in eastern Europe, German Jews were an integral part of the country. They spoke German like other Germans, wore the same clothes and lived in the same houses. They were at one with the surrounding population. There was nothing in their lifestyle to distinguish them from Germans who were not Jewish.

I grew up in the midst of anti-Semitic events day after day. Aware of the unceasing sense of insecurity of the adults, I overheard the worried, concerned conversations my parents had with their friends. How long would this last? Would it escalate? What should we do? The key issue was always: should we stay or should we leave? Nobody had a definitive answer. In these whispered conversations nothing was resolved.

I saw what the Nazi press printed: Jews were terrible, threatening, destructive, dishonest, unethical, ugly, communist, capitalist, criminal. On my way home from school, I walked by the showcases that displayed these papers for the public to read. They were everywhere. The worst of them was the rabidly anti-Semitic "Stürmer." I could see people who bought and read the "Stürmer" with great interest. The text was accompanied by hideous caricatures of Jews with long noses, ugly faces, fat paunches—Jews committing evil, unspeakable acts. I often stopped at the showcases to take a look. What I saw in these caricatures was not me, nor anybody else I knew. But what was shown was not intended for me. It was meant to incite the Aryan citizens of Germany against me, my family and my friends.

I walked by an increasing number of establishments that displayed signs in their doors and windows that said *"Juden nicht erwünscht"* ("Jews not desired," which really meant "Jews not allowed.") I saw them in cafes, restaurants, movie houses, waiting rooms, train stations, at the zoo and at the entrance of entire villages. I obeyed them. My life, and that of my parents and brother, and of all other Jews became ever more restricted. My parents could no longer take me to the zoo, nor could they go out on weekends to have the *Kaffee und Kuchen* (coffee and cake) that had been such a beloved tradition. They could no longer go to the movies, the theater or to concerts. All that disappeared from our lives.

I was afraid of the Storm Troopers who constantly marched in the streets. I saw them when I went to school, when I came home and when I went to visit friends. There was no escape. I had to listen to the *"Horst Wessel Lied,"* the real anthem of the Nazis, named after the son of a Protestant chaplain who had gone to live in the slums of Berlin with a former prostitute to fight for the Nazi cause.

Wessel was killed in a brawl with Communists in 1930 and transformed into a martyr by the Nazis. He had written a song that called for raising the flag and closing ranks, that the *SA*, the Storm Troopers, were marching in quest of their Nazi goals. Other songs threatened the destruction of the Jews, celebrating the day when Jewish blood would drip from their knives and then everything would be better (for Germany), while yet others proclaimed that while Germany belonged to them today, tomorrow it would be the whole world. As children we listened to these hate-filled songs every day. We'd hear them in the streets and on the radio. I began to question myself whether they were right, whether I was inferior because I was a Jew.

The relentless insistence on the inferiority of the Jews and the superiority of the Aryans had an impact on me. Often, I asked myself if it was really true that I was less worthy. The Nazi propaganda machine, designed to teach the Aryan population to hate their Jewish neighbors, could not fail to have an impact on the young, unformed minds of the targets of this propaganda. What was there in a child's mind to counteract constantly repeated assertions of inferiority?

I had a frequently recurring nightmare that reflected my anxieties. I saw myself standing at a small beach, flanked on the left side by a massive dune. As I entered the water, the dune would topple over and bury me. I went to bed at night dreading this dream, knowing that it would recur again and again. I was not a particularly religious child, but in my anxiety I started to pray. When I was very little, my mother taught me to pray that my heart remain pure and that nobody should reside in it but God. Millions of other German children learned that prayer. Later, when I was a bit older, I was taught "*Shmah Yisrael*" (Hear, oh Israel), the holiest of Jewish prayers. But in 1937 I wanted none of that. Something else was on my mind. My prayer was "Dear God, please save us. Please let us get us out of here. Please let us escape." After Crystal Night my prayers became more urgent, and although there was no answer, they gave me hope and I slept.

One day in 1936 I stood at an open window in my father's office at the factory and watched another parade. This one was special. Hitler had come to visit Königsberg. The caravan moved down the main street where I had watched the Nazi May Day parade two years earlier. The *Führer* stood in an open car, raising his hand in the Nazi salute, smiling at the jubilant crowds. I heard the *SA* shouting for Jews to close their windows. But the non-Jewish employees wanted to watch and the windows remained open. Not only that, but Nazi Storm Troopers came up and asked to watch from our windows. It was terrifying, but they could not be denied. The Jewish owners, the non-Jewish employees, and the uniformed Nazis all crowded together at the windows as if they were the best of friends. The scene would have been laughable, had it not been so serious. The fear was palpable, but no one said a word—not the Jews, not the employees, not the Nazis.

During those years in Königsberg there were always people leaving—going to Palestine, to America, to other countries. It became a natural, expected event to lose family and friends. I sensed that those who left had escaped the dark, undefined fate that was looming in my future. My favorite cousin, Lola, left for Palestine. She was my role model, the ideal who inspired me. She had helped me when I had difficulties with my parents by standing up for me, and she had prevailed on them to let me join a Zionist youth group. I missed her deeply. (Sadly, she died at a young age, and I never saw her again.) The leader of my Zionist youth group went to America, leaving a void that could not be filled because so many other young people had also departed. The youth group had to be disbanded. My cousins Martin and Curt left for Argentina. My mother's younger sister, Aunt Ella, left for Palestine with her whole family. There was a little girl, Judith Wolff, who was in my class at school. She was so pretty that I could not take my eyes off her. We played together, and I was in love with her. She left too, and I missed her. The circle of family and friends grew ever smaller, but my parents made no move to leave. Their wake-up call had not yet sounded.

At school we filed into the large common room every Friday for the celebration of the "Sabbath Hour," held just before school let out for the week. It was an occasion to sing and for student performances of various kinds. As time went on, it also became a poignant occasion to bid farewell to departing friends. The school's principal pinned a little red ribbon on each departing student's chest, a "heart string" to remind them that they were part of those who remained behind, and not to forget us, but to keep in touch. It was also a time to read the letters from those who were already gone. I was sad to see my friends leave, but at the same time I had the sense that they were being saved from a horrible future that had already begun to take shape. I was also envious, and asked myself why my parents failed to join the exodus.

What were my parents thinking? They were intelligent, well-informed people. They knew what was happening. They heard warnings from their non-Jewish friends. But they were German to the core. If not anti-Zionist, they were at least indifferent to the idea of building a Jewish homeland in Palestine. Their homeland was Germany. Twenty years earlier my father had gone to war for Germany, and he had been decorated for that by the German Army in 1935—two years after Hitler came to power! My parents were certainly not alone in their allegiance to Germany. The leadership of the liberal congregation did not encourage us to leave, and the highly respected rabbi, Reinhold Lewin, fiercely rejected Zionism as incompatible with being a loyal German citizen.

My father belonged to an organization called the "Central Association of German Citizens of the Jewish Faith" (CV for short), which had been founded in 1893 to combat anti-Semitism in Germany. In 1933 its membership comprised 60% of the Jewish families.[5] Its goal was to fuse Jewish culture with the broader German culture. In April of 1933 a veteran CV leader, Alfred Hirschberg, exhorted readers of the "CV Zeitung" (CV journal) that "it is our aim to preserve within Germany a German Jewish community, unbroken financially, physically and spiritually."[6] The conflict between the assimilationist CV and the Zionists, which had started before World War 1, remained constant even in those years of increasing anti-Semitic measures that limited the economic, social and cultural lives of German Jews and imposed stringent measures on them.

In hindsight it is difficult to understand how so many Jews were so mistaken: how they disregarded all the threats, the virulent anti-Jewish propaganda, the Nuremberg racial laws of 1935, the curtailment of Jewish professional activities and the physical violence. But the influential CV, fighting for the preservation of Jewish rights as citizens in Germany, reinforced the identification with German culture and the sense that the Jews were part of Germany. The influence exerted by the CV—through their publications, meetings, and, in Königsberg, through the advice of the rabbi—prevented many Jews from realizing that things had radically changed, that their assumptions were no longer valid. The "CV Zeitung" told readers that "Germany will remain Germany and nobody can rob us of our homeland and our fatherland." Until very late, the CV section in Königsberg appealed to its members to remain in Germany.[7] The influence of the CV convinced many Jews that there was no need to leave, that things would eventually get better.

My assimilated father's opinion was, "Give Hitler enough rope and he will hang himself." Of course, there was a successful business enterprise that tied my parents down. Not only did it provide them with a good income, but it was their creation, their main accomplishment in life. Moreover, they were not young. In 1936 my father was fifty-two years old, my mother fifty. There were some dis-

---

[5] Lucy S. Davidowicz, The War Against the Jews 1933–1945, Holt, Rinehart and Winston, May 1975.
[6] Ibid.
[7] Stefanie Schüler-Springorum, "Die jüdische Minderheit in Königsberg/Preussen, 1871–1945," Vandenhoeck & Ruprecht, 1996.

cussions in our house. There was the possibility of moving to Holland. When my parents talked about it I understood why they did not want to leave. They agreed that no harm would come. They were Germans. The Nazis could not put their threats into action. They would not last. There was no need to uproot the business and family. Then, in 1937 there was an opportunity to emigrate to Chile. They rehashed the same arguments, and my mother settled the matter with one sentence, "To that earthquake country? Never!"

In 1935 my mother's younger sister and her family decided to leave for Palestine. They came for a farewell Passover meal—*Tante* Ella, the sister, her husband, and their two daughters, Ruth aged nine and Else, a few years older. It was the first time I met this branch of the family, and I immediately made friends with Ruth. We prepared the traditional four questions to be asked by the youngest participant at the Passover meal, the *seder.* The conversation about the impending move started that evening. Initially they talked only of what the visitors were planning to do once they got to Palestine. They planned to open a restaurant in a new town, Nahariya, which in time became a center for Jewish immigrants from Germany. From that night on until our relatives left the debate continued in our house. Much of what was said I did not understand because I was too young. But I did understand that my assimilated parents felt safe, and that our Zionist relatives did not and were trying to convince my parents that they were wrong. Similar conversations were taking place among Jews all over Germany. The question, simply put, was: Is this an aberration? A temporary insanity? Or is disaster awaiting those who refuse to flee? Today we know the answer: it was not clear then.

Two events from my childhood illustrate the sense of the times. My mother's older sister lived in Germau, a small village near Königsberg. It was a two-hour train ride away. My aunt and uncle ran a general store that sold everything the villagers needed in their daily lives: clothing, dishes, stationary and tools. Whenever I went to visit, I spent my days among the fruit trees and bushes behind the store where there were two acres of open land, and at night I slept in the living quarters above the store. Upon my arrival at the train station near Germau, I'd take a bus to the store, or, if the weather was good, I'd walk, which took about twenty minutes. Along the way, I'd pass through fields lined with trees—green and flowery in the summer, and white with snow in the winter, and then come by a church and a graveyard on the outskirts of Germau. In the very center of the village stood the store. My aunt and uncle and their four children were the only Jews.

Their family frequently visited us in Königsberg, and I spent many happy days in Germau. One day in 1935, I was traveling to Germau with my parents.

After we changed trains in the small village of Fischhausen, I entered the new compartment, which was shared with other travelers, and I loudly said, *"Heil, Genosse Stalin!"* (Hail, Comrade Stalin!) The Nazi era was in full swing and anyone suspected of communist sympathies was sent to a concentration camp. Where I had heard that expression, I don't know. Fortunately the other passengers did not react, and there was not a *Gestapo* or Nazi party official among them. My parents were terrified for the remainder of the trip, and I was severely reprimanded after we arrived. But at the age of seven years old, I did not understand the danger that I had placed us in; however, I quickly internalized this lesson.

On another occasion, I went walking along the piers by the river where the large ships docked. I liked to look at the ships and watch the cranes unloading the cargo at the old warehouses. I frequently went there by myself, and I dreamed of sailing away to far-off places. One day as I sat at the edge of the water, I was joined by another boy and we started talking. He was not Jewish and just talking to him was an unusual event. We commented on how each of our respective families was being persecuted by the Nazis. The boy's family was *Bibelforscher* (Jehovah's Witness), a sect almost as despised as the Jews. I told the boy my name, and by the time I got home it was already dark. I told my parents about the conversation with this non-Jewish boy who felt like we did about Hitler and the Nazis. They were terror-stricken. If this boy had gone home to his parents and told them about the conversation, the consequences could be severe. What if his parents denounced us to the *Gestapo*? Fortunately, nothing happened and I never saw that boy again. But, for a second time, I had put the family in serious jeopardy.

The Factory

My parents owned a rainwear factory, and they also operated a small fur coat business that had been founded by my grandparents. These two businesses provided our family with a good income.

My father and a partner had opened the rainwear factory in 1924. It was registered under the name of *Ostpreussische Regenmäntelfabrik* (East Prussian Raincoat Factory), or ORFA for short. From the beginning my father was the manager of the business. In 1930 his partner left and my father became the sole owner. Initially, the factory employed twenty people, but the workforce quickly grew to forty. Having outgrown the original building, a new one was built. ORFA continued to grow, until ultimately 100 workers were employed. Prior to the onset of modern mass production methods, this was a good-sized enterprise. Approximately two-thirds of the company products were sold in Germany; not only to commercial retail establishments but my father also had a large contract to supply the German Army with rainwear. The factory also produced products for export, primarily to Sweden, Lithuania and Czechoslovakia. Annual sales were approximately 700,00 Marks (or about three million dollars in 1994 value). The business was important to the Army and the government remained a major customer well past the time when other Jewish enterprises were boycotted. The rainwear factory, but not the fur business, was "aryanized" in August 1938, which meant that ownership was officially transferred to a non-Jewish German citizen. This was a transfer in name only and allowed the Army to continue to do business with ORFA after the anti-Jewish laws had been passed. In reality, my parents continued to own and manage the business.

Offices and showrooms occupied the second floor of the building at *Vorstädtische Langgasse* 103. On the other two floors were rented apartments. From the rear of the building, a block-long yard led to the factory where the coats were made. Sometimes after school I visited my parents in their offices. Mother was the bookkeeper and financial officer of the firm and shared her office with the head clerk. As I entered her office I passed by a large black safe on my left. I remember this safe well because it would later play a critical role in our lives.

Usually it was early afternoon when I arrived at the factory. Mother would be sitting at her desk working on the accounting books, and I'd tell her about my day at school, show her my homework and sometimes my grades. One day I begged her to let me learn to swim in a public pool where swimming lessons were being given. I had to convince her that I really wanted and needed to learn how to swim. She finally agreed and gave me the money to pay the instructor. I raced to our home a few blocks away, dumped my school bag, grabbed my bathing suit, and ran to the pool where I started my lessons with the friendly *Bademeister* (pool manager). In the summer of 1936 Jews were still allowed to swim in the public pools. The *Bademeister* was nice to me. He taught me well, and in no time I earned my certificate as a "free swimmer." To earn the certificate I had to swim the breaststroke for twenty minutes while the *Bademeister* stood watching, stop watch in hand. When the time was up, he hollered for me to stop. Young children were required to have this certificate to swim in the deep side of the pool, and I was very happy.

Mother's assistant, the head clerk, was a dedicated Nazi who arrived at work dressed in the brown uniform of the Storm Troopers. He had been employed at ORFA for a long time, and my parents thought he was a good worker. Even though they were uncomfortable having him there in his uniform, it was impossible to fire him. His name was *Herr* Meyer. He was a key actor in the drama that led to our family's last-minute escape from Germany. Beyond the office was a large showroom for the raincoats. The windows where we had watched Hitler were at the end of this room. Frequently, this was where I would find my father when I came to the factory after school. If he wasn't there, I'd look in one of the smaller showrooms where the furs were displayed. Sometimes I'd see him, cigarette in hand, talking to a man I did not know. I always thought it was strange because my father was a non-smoker. I later learned that the man was an important customer, and whenever he offered my father a cigarette he accepted it to be polite. But he never knew quite what to do with it.

One day I entered my father's office with an important question on my mind. The school principal's wife had a new baby. I was seven- or eight-years-old, and I wanted to know where babies came from. So in class at school I'd asked the principal, "How did that happen?" I had no idea, and neither did any of the other children. We all wanted to know. But the principal was shocked by this unexpected question and obviously embarrassed. He didn't answer. He just mumbled something that we couldn't understand. So after school, I ran off to find my father. I found him in his showroom sorting some merchandise. I interrupted what he was doing and put my question to him, confident that he would give me a proper answer. Very seriously my father took my hand and marched me to a window located on a landing between two floors. At the window he explained that if a couple wanted a child, they would put a lump of sugar on a window sill just like the one we were looking at. The stork would fly by, see that the couple wanted to have a baby, and then bring it. "How," I asked, "does the stork know if the parents want a boy or a girl?" My father replied that if the lump of sugar was large, it would mean the stork should bring a boy, and if it was small the stork would bring a girl. Of course, I knew right away that this was not true, and I felt bad. My father had betrayed the trust I had in him. Since there was nobody else to ask I remained ignorant on that subject for many more years.

An equally amusing story was told to me by Judith, my puppy love, when I met her again many years later. She asked her mother a similar question when they were walking by a store selling lottery tickets. Her mother told her that she had been won by one of the lottery tickets; she was the top prize of that particular drawing. Judith and I later argued about who was right—my father or her mother. We never resolved the question to our mutual satisfaction.

It was an adventure when I went to the factory building instead of to the offices. I entered a large workshop with rows and rows of sewing machines, cutting tables and other work areas. The seamstresses all knew me. Sometimes one or another would take me on her lap and show me what she was doing. I don't know what it did to their production quotas, but they were willing to take a little time to entertain the boss' son. At some tables they covered the coat seams with rubber to make them waterproof. At other tables they sewed on buttons or made button holes. There was no end to the wonders I saw. A Jewish woman named *Frau* Marwilski was the supervisor. Her daughter, Ruth, was one of my classmates. They lived in a tiny apartment across the street from the factory. I was fond of *Frau* Marwilski. She was always friendly and I thought she liked me. Ruth and I liked each other too. I often ended an afternoon in the factory by crossing the street to the Marwilski's apartment, where I was given milk and cookies and I played with Ruth.

Other adventures awaited when I went to the yard. There was a house and some storage sheds on one side. A custodian lived in the house with his daughter, who was year or two older than I. On the other side of the wall across from the house stood the orthodox Old Synagogue. One day it caught fire. I looked out one of the office windows and saw smoke coming out of the roof of the synagogue. I shouted and one of our office employees called the fire department. In no time at all, big fire trucks arrived. I watched the firemen put out the flames, which fortunately seemed to be confined to the roof only. It was an exciting show, but I was glad when, after an hour or so, it was over. Against the same wall on the side of the yard there were two cages, really just two wooden boxes, where my brother and I kept our two rabbits. Each rabbit had its own cage. Together we went out to open fields in the neighborhood and collected plants, especially dandelions, to feed them. Sometimes we cleaned the cages. It was a messy task and the cages stank, so we did it as rarely as possible. We'd put both rabbits together in one cage, remove the wet straw, excrement, and other filth, and wash the cage, then fill it with the fresh straw that had been supplied by the custodian. Then we'd repeat the operation with the other cage. More often than not we evaded the task and it was the custodian who took care of the rabbits. They would have starved and succumbed in their own filth if left to the mercy of two boys! I don't know how we came by those rabbits. Maybe my parents thought it would teach us responsibility and they asked the custodian, who had his own rabbits in another part of the yard, to supply these two. The rabbits did not teach us anything. They weren't even any fun.

The greatest adventure the yard had to offer was to play with the custodian's daughter. That was because she was the only non-Jewish child I ever played with during my childhood in Germany. It was only possible because the yard was enclosed, and nobody could see us unless they looked down from the windows in the office. Together, we ran all over the yard playing the usual children's games—catch, hide-and-seek, marbles and tag, or sometimes we played forbidden games in the storage sheds. At other times she helped me take care of the rabbits; a task at which she was more adept than I.

The New Apartment

I was seven years old. Big changes were taking place. I was going to the Jewish school, our two maids had been dismissed, and we no longer lived on the noisy main street but in a new apartment on a quiet, tree-lined street. The two former maids had to be dismissed because they were "too young." According to the Nazi racial laws of 1935, Jews were not allowed to employ female servants under the age of forty-five. My parents hired an older woman named Anna who was safely beyond that age. The new apartment was around the corner from where we had previously lived, a block from the main street, and three blocks from the factory. The apartment was on *Kaiserstrasse*, the "street of the emperor," and located in a house similar to the other middle-class houses that lined the street. Our apartment was on the ground floor. There were two other floors in the house, each with one apartment, topped by an attic where on wash days the laundry was dried.

Anna was hired as a maid, but she also performed other duties. The running of the business left my parents little time for raising children. So Anna had to care for us when we were home from school, and she served as a substitute mother. I think my parents, and in particular my mother, lacked the inclination and understanding necessary to bring up children. Consequently, as my brother and I grew older, our relationship with our parents was never close.

When I came home from school, I always found Anna in the kitchen. Mother was never home. I did not mind as I liked Anna. She fed me cookies, cake and warm milk, and we talked about my school day. I also went to the kitchen at other times during the day just to be with Anna. After my snack I crossed the hall to my room, which I shared with my brother. He came home later than I did, and for a while I had the room to myself where I could play or do homework.

It was different on Fridays. All Jewish holidays, including the Sabbath, begin on the prior evening, and that made Friday special in our house. Mother often stayed home from work to prepare the traditional "gefilte fish." She'd go to the nearby open air market early in the morning to buy the fish and then painstakingly skin, clean, grind and cook it. The task required most of her day. I looked forward to the result of her labor, the fish and the soup, which we ate in the evening. No gefilte fish I've ever had was as good as the gefilte fish Mother knew how to make.

Sometimes I accompanied my mother to the open air market to buy the fish, where she also bought chickens, vegetables, fruit, butter and cheese. She'd walk from stand to stand and finger the fish and the chicken to make sure they were fresh, and she'd taste the cheeses and check the butter to make sure it was not rancid. She'd haggle with the farmwives and fish women, who all spoke in the picturesque dialect peculiar to our region that was impossible for an outsider to understand. While she haggled at one stand, the seller at the next stand would try to lure her over by claiming that her merchandisè was superior. I thought the haggling, the competition, the smells and the shouting were fun, but at times I felt a bit embarrassed. I didn't need to because it was the traditional way of doing business. Every housewife in the crowded market behaved exactly as my mother did. After we left the market, we'd go to the Jewish butcher where Mother bought the beef that Anna would boil for the Saturday midday meal. The boiled beef was traditional, but it was also tough and tasteless, and I never ate again after I had grown up and left my parents' home.

For the Sabbath evening meal, the dining room table was set with special plates on a gleaming white tablecloth, and with silverware engraved with the family initial "F." Two Sabbath candleholders with unlit candles stood on the table. Two traditional, twisted Sabbath breads, called *challah,* were placed on a cutting board beneath a special cover. A silver cup for the ritual wine stood next to my father's chair. We often had guests, and my aunt and uncle from Germau were frequent visitors. Rarely did we eat alone on the Sabbath.

After Mother lit the candles, my father recited the *kiddush* prayer and said the blessings over the wine and bread. Everybody tasted the wine, including the children, and then pieces of *challah* were distributed to all. After that, we were ready to eat. Anna came in and served the meal. I was impatient for the tasty soup with broth made from boiling the fish, as well as the gefilte fish itself. I cared less for the chicken and vegetables that followed. The meal was finished with whatever desert Anna had prepared. After we were through eating, I happily accompanied my father in singing the many melodies of the traditional prayer he recited after the meal.

When the meal was over, we moved into the adjoining salon which had an armchair in one corner, and a desk, a piano, and a bookcase that lined an entire wall. I joined the company as they sat around the coffee table and talked. As always, they were worried about their businesses. But now more and more often

I became aware of a note of fear creeping into the conversations. I was conditioned to this fear. I felt it myself every day.

When my parents were not home and I could not fall asleep, I went to Anna's room. It was narrow, with barely enough space for a bed, dresser and chair. Whenever I was anxious about something that had happened during the day—an incident on the streets, something I had observed or read or a scolding by my mother—just being with Anna calmed me. After a while, I'd be ready to go back to my own room.

Besides cooking and cleaning, Anna did all the laundry. She did it by hand, and used a machine to squeeze excess moisture out of the freshly laundered bed linen and towels. On laundry days I accompanied her to the attic and helped her hang the laundry to dry. Anna was very busy, but I think she was fond of me and I always felt secure in her company.

Anna woke me every morning in time to get ready for school. To start the day, I crossed the hall to the bathroom where we had little squares of cut up newspaper hanging next to the toilet instead of toilet paper. I'd seen such paper in the bathrooms of other houses. It was a custom used by many frugal Germans. I do not remember if the newspaper was exchanged for something more appropriate when guests were expected. I washed and brushed my teeth hoping that Mother would not come in and take her shower while I was there, as she frequently did. There was no shower curtain, and I was always embarrassed by the sight of her in the shower. I'd hurry though my bathroom chores, hoping that she would stay in bed until after I was done. After I was dressed and had breakfast, I headed out the door to school.

There were two ways I could go. After leaving the house, I could turn to the right, cross the main street, and follow *Kaiserstrasse* about five blocks to a dead-end, where I turned left on *Lindenstrasse* and walked another five blocks to the synagogue. Sometimes I picked up a friend who lived along the way. It was a safe route, but it was also boring. The other way was a more exciting way to go. Instead of crossing the main street, I'd turn left and walk past the stock exchange and then cross the *Grüne Brücke* (the Green Bridge) over the Pregel river. The bridge frequently opened to let ships pass through. When that happened, all traffic came to a stop—cars, horse carts, streetcars and pedestrians. After a few minutes the bridge closed and we'd continue on our way. This bridge provided a perfect excuse if I'd dawdled along the way and was late to school. All I had to say was that the bridge was open and then all was well. After crossing the bridge, I turned right and walked along the quays, crossed another bridge, the *Honig-*

brücke (the Honey Bridge), over another arm of the river that led to the synagogue now directly in front of me. Lining the quays were century old warehouses, narrow buildings four or five stories high. Their stairs were too narrow to raise or lower the goods they were intended to store, so a different method had been devised. Every warehouse had a pulley just below the roof. Packages of great bulk were raised up or brought down by ropes and cables running through the pulleys. The loads were moved in and out of the buildings through bulkheads on each floor. Boats arrived in the morning and I'd watch as fish from the Baltic Sea or produce from the provinces was unloaded onto waiting horse carts and trucks. The goods were offered for sale that same day in the various open air markets in the city. A little further on, but a bit out of my way, large freighters were tied up bringing goods from other countries and loading freight to be taken back.

One morning I looked up and saw one of the two German zeppelins, a rigid airship called after its inventor, Count von Zeppelin. The zeppelins transported passengers across the Atlantic to America. Now, as this one glided silently above the river, it caused a sensation. A zeppelin had never come to Königsberg before. A few months later, in May of 1937, the zeppelin Hindenburg caught fire and burned while landing at Lakehurst, New Jersey, in far-off America, killing thirty-six of its passengers and crew. That ended the use of these airships for transatlantic passenger transportation. I'd also see divers in heavy copper helmets and diving suits with large ballast weights attached so they could explore the river floor—for what reason, I do not know. They operated from barges anchored in the river. I watched, fascinated, as the divers put on their helmets and lowered themselves into the water with hoses and lifelines secured on the barges. Two men on board rhythmically pumped air to them with a manual pump. When the divers came back up, the two men stopped pumping and helped the divers remove their helmets and ballast weights.

I loved to take this route to and from school because every morning and every afternoon was different. It was a child's dream world, an ever changing picture of ships and barges, the unloading of vegetable and fish, the sounds of peasant dialects and the smells of the river and the quays. But it was also dangerous. It was here, along the river, that I was most often taunted by groups of non-Jewish boys. Sometimes I was the target of their stones. When I took this route, I was forever watchful. Boys dressed in the uniform of the Hitler Youth might suddenly surge from behind a doorway or a truck and run after me. I was lucky if they only shouted insults. They called me names like *Dreckjude* (dirty Jew), or *Saujude* (loosely translated as "sow's Jew"), which was a typical German insult. But sometimes their attacks were more vicious. They would rush at me with stones in their hands, throwing the stones as they shouted their insults, while I ran, desperately trying to dodge the flying rocks.

Sometimes I went to the *Schlossteich* (the Castle Lake) located just behind the castle. When I was younger, *Fräulein* Martha took me there in the summer to play. I saw young couples, nursemaids with their charges trailing after them and students promenading along the paths by the lake and over the bridge that crossed it. But in winter, when the lake was frozen, I looked forward to skating. The lake was still open to me, as the *"Juden nicht erwünscht"* sign did not go up until after the 1937 winter season. On holidays or in the afternoon after school, I'd walk to the *Grüne Brücke*, but instead of turning, I'd continue straight on and cross the *Krämer Brücke* (the Bridge of the Tradesmen) over the second Pregel arm to the *Kaiser-Wilhelm-Platz* (the Emperor William Square) in front of the castle. Two monuments gave the square its martial character. One was a statue of the 19th century chancellor Bismarck, the "Iron Chancellor," who succeeded in his ambition to unify Germany, and the other was a statue of Emperor Wilhelm I, who had been King of Prussia and then the emperor of the unified Germany in Bismarck's time. Past the square and the castle, I'd turn right on *Schlosstrasse* (Castle Street) for one block to reach the entrance of the skating area on the lake. I'd pay the fee of a few Pfennig, and put my skates on in a room with wooden benches. Using a key, I tightened the skate brackets around the soles of my shoes. I skated in my everyday clothes. Although I was not a good skater, I could keep my balance in the circle with the others skaters on the ice. When it got dark, I'd take off my skates, hang them around my neck and start home. At night I'd take a different route though the old part of the city, past the fish market and the coal market, which were closed and silent. On several street corners I'd see uniformed Storm Troopers collecting money for the *Winterhilfswerk,* a project to provide winter aid for poor people. They encouraged passersby to purchase lottery tickets. A one-mark ticket could pay five or ten marks, but most often paid nothing. Buyers not only wanted to win, they also wanted to help their needy fellow citizens. Unfortunately, it was later discovered that the money collected was not given to the poor but diverted to the state, much of it was probably spent on the purchase of arms. I frequently watched as the Storm Troopers sold their tickets, but I rarely had any money. On a couple of occasions, however, I did have enough to buy a lottery ticket. I never won. Beyond the markets, I passed an *Automat*, a sandwich store where one could insert a few coins into a slot next to a small window, whereupon the window would miraculously open to offer a delectable sandwich of cheese, ham and salami, or liverwurst with bits of bacon that was a specialty of our region. I loved to eat one of those sandwiches while I warmed up from the freezing temperatures on the lake. But most of the time I had no money for this pleasure, and I had to pass by this paradise and wait for dinner at home.

My Life in the Family

My mother was my father's second wife. Still single into his late thirties, his mother forced him, for business reasons, into a loveless marriage; although he loved another woman and had already committed to marry her. The first marriage failed after nineteen months. Only then did he marry my mother, who was the woman he loved. After I learned of his first marriage, I wondered if I had any unknown half-siblings anywhere. But, there were no children from that first marriage. In those years divorce was shameful, and my parents never told me of my father's first marriage. In fact, they denied it even after I had found incontrovertible proof of it.

At the outset of their marriage, my parents observed many of the religious rules. They ate kosher meat, keeping separate dishes for milk and meat meals. Additional dishes were used for the Passover holiday. They had four sets of dishes in all. But that was before I was born. By the time I had arrived, they had abandoned some of the traditional religious customs. They no longer used separate dishes for milk and meat. Even though we didn't eat kosher meals, pork and other forbidden foods never entered the house, and they still kept the separate Passover dishes which were stored in a trunk in the attic. Just before Passover the trunk was brought down to the apartment, and we all helped unpack the dishes, the silverware, the pots and pans and the kitchen utensils. The trunk was then repacked with the everyday counterparts and returned to the attic. Eight days later, at the end of the holiday, we reversed the process.

Passover celebrates the exodus of the Israelites from captive slavery in Egypt, and it is a celebration of freedom. The older I became, the more I was aware of our own enslavement in Germany. In my mind, the commemoration of freedom gained in the exodus was transformed into a prayer for freedom *now*. The first two nights were celebrated at home in a traditional ritual meal called the *seder* (the order) because everything proceeds in a prescribed way with little variation year after year. I loved the Passover holiday because of its rich tradition, and I felt a closeness to the family I did not feel at other times. The idea of freedom that Passover commemorated touched something deep inside me at a time when I felt increasingly anxious about the tyranny that had begun to dominate our lives in Nazi Germany.

For the Passover *seder*, the table in the dining room was prepared much like on Friday evenings, except there were other plates. Instead of *challah* there was a plate of unleavened bread known as *matzah*, which was the only bread we were allowed to eat during the eight days of Passover. There was a plate with ritual objects: a shank bone, an egg, ground apples prepared with nuts and wine, a vegetable and herbs. My father recited various blessings he read from the *Haggada*, the special prayer book used for the *seder* that recounts the Jewish exodus from Egypt. The ritual and the readings were the same both evenings. Year after year I heard the identical words in Hebrew and in German. As the youngest participant, I recited and sang four ritual questions about the difference of that particular evening from all the other evenings of the year. While I sang, the attention of the whole assembly, my parents and ten or fifteen guests was focused on me. After my part was over, my father read answers from the *Haggada*. Other family members and guests read parts of the book, some of which were sung with traditional melodies reserved for the *seder*. Finally, an extensive meal was served. But that was not the end. After the meal we said more prayers. I sung them with the other participants. By this time, four glasses of ritual wine had been emptied. My glass was small, but even so, at the end of the evening I was slightly drunk. The ritual ended with the fervent wish, "Next Year in Jerusalem." For most, it was just a wish. The British tightly controlled the certificates needed to go to Palestine, and nowhere near enough were provided to accommodate all of those who wanted and needed them. My own thoughts were mostly "next year, elsewhere." I didn't care where, I just wanted to be far, far away.

On summer Sundays we traveled to a suburban garden cafe in a nearby village called Metgheten to enjoy the traditional German *Kaffee und Kuchen* at a garden table under the trees. I liked to run and play in the nearby woods to gather blueberries and to admire wild flowers that I did not see in the city. But I would not do so until after I had eaten some *Apfelstrudel mit Schlagsahne* (apple pie smothered in heavy cream) and had a cup of hot chocolate. I'd spend the afternoon running around among the trees in the meadow. If I became thirsty, I'd return to my parent's table in the cafe for a glass of lemonade and maybe some ice cream. The other children did likewise. It was always fun, and at the end of the day I didn't mind when the train was overcrowded and we had to spend the half-hour return trip pressed together like sardines in a can.

On winter Sundays, my parents liked to go to cafes in the city. Plouda was my favorite. When we entered we were shown to a table by a formally dressed waiter. The chairs were plush, the table linen spotless and the silver gleaming in the light of the chandeliers. Hot chocolate appeared in front of me as if by magic, along with cake and cookies and, most important, marzipan. Königsberg marzipan was famous in Germany and in many other countries, and Plouda's was the most famous of all. When I brought home a particularly good report card from school, my reward was a little box of Plouda's marzipan. I could not think of anything better. But one day, I think it was in 1937, as we approached Plouda, we stopped. At the entrance I saw a big sign which said "*Juden nicht erwünscht.*" At other nearby cafes the same signs were hanging in the door. My parents gave up and we went home. From that day forward, more and more signs appeared at the entrances of business and public establishments. Sadly, there were no more summer excursions. There was no more hot chocolate, no more marzipan and no more *Kuchen.*

I was never close to my mother. I do not know why, but can only speculate. Perhaps it was that she was so much older than I, and so old fashioned. Most of my friends' mothers were younger. Perhaps she was more preoccupied with the business than with her children. I was not alone in feeling that way. My brother felt the same. As I grew older, I heard her friends and acquaintances say how much they respected her for her helpfulness, for her cultural interests and for the advice she gave. But they frequently added that she was a difficult woman to deal with. I never felt the same admiration and respect that her friends expressed. Instead, I felt that she wanted to dominate me and impose her will on me. I was a stubborn child. She could not accept that and did not understand how to handle a child with an independent mind. We clashed all the time, and our difficulties intensified as I grew older. I was disobedient and spiteful, and was known as a child out of control. In retrospect, I think that with more understanding and more respect from her for the person I was, Mother and I could have avoided our conflicts. I did not behave in the same way with my father who accepted me for who I was.

One day, when I was seven years old, Mother and I were walking along the main street doing some shopping. She met a friend and started talking and the conversation turned to their children. I stood patiently listening while the other woman described the accomplishments of her children. With a significant look at me, my mother said, "But you, you have good children." The implication was clear. Mother had made that remark as a way of letting me know, yet again, that I was not a good child. I was deeply hurt and I never forgot the incident.

I often came home from home school with severe stomach cramps. They would get so bad that I'd bend over in pain and last for many hours. Anna was busy with her chores and could offer sympathy, but no help. I'd pick up the phone and call my mother at her office three blocks away. Sometimes she was too busy to come to the phone. If she did, all she would say was that the pain would go away. I knew that, but I needed her there to comfort me. At such times I felt sad and thought that she did not love me.

Mother was a career woman in an age when this was not customary. She had little time to provide her children the attention they craved, and I envied my friends when I played at their houses. Their mothers were at home, and they would give us snacks and talk to us. It seemed to me as if my mother was the only mother who was never home.

Her attempts to control my life never ceased—not when I was a teenager, not when I was an adult, not when I married and not when I had children of my own. I understood what her friends meant when they said that she was a difficult woman. She scolded and wept when she was crossed or her wishes went unfulfilled. She tried to make me feel guilty over issues large and small, and she often said that my behavior would kill her ("bring her under the earth" translated from the German expression she used). At other times, she would use gifts to try and put me under her obligation. She did the same with relatives and friends, and then complained that the recipients of these gifts (including God) were ungrateful when her expectations were not met. On some occasions, when she looked back over her life or when she was ill, she would say that she had donated so much money to the synagogue and had done so many good deeds that she expected God to take care of her. Since He had not, all her efforts had been in vain.

I regret that my relationship with my mother was so difficult. As an adult, I read poems and stories written by men who praised their mothers and expressed a deep love for them. Intellectually, I accepted these sentiments, but I was never able to share them on an emotional level. I've always felt deprived.

On Sunday mornings I enjoyed getting up early to share my father's breakfast with him: soft boiled eggs, bread and jam. Mother would still be asleep, and after breakfast Father would take my hand and we'd walk to the post office near the main railway station, the *Hauptbahnhof*, to pick up mail. We walked down a street with a strange name, *Knochenstrasse*, the Street of Bones. It took perhaps half an hour to get to the post office. I don't remember what we talked about, but when we came home I always felt happy and content.

Father had relatively little formal education. He had become an apprentice at the age of fourteen, as was common practice at the end of the 19th century when he was growing up. At meals, he'd talk about business, the day's events, the threatening political situation and family matters. Some evenings my parents went to the theater. My mother would urge him to go even when he was reluctant, but I never heard him talk about the theater at home. Music and the arts were never discussed, except for the novels that he was fond of reading. He was very "old-fashioned." His morals were those of the previous century, and he never changed. One evening when I was already a teenager, I brought my girlfriend home for a sandwich. It was ten o'clock and both my parents were there, yet the next morning Father took me aside and told me that I had compromised my girlfriend's reputation and that I should never do such a thing again.

In later years I thought about my father's relationship with his mother and his wife. I saw him as a person in need of support from whoever was closest to him during the various periods of his life. He was dominated first by his mother, then my mother did the same. It seemed to me that in this respect he had married a woman just like his mother in order to fill some unfulfilled need.

I dislike literary or operatic male characters who are weak and vacillating in their relations with women, such as Don Ottavio in Mozart's opera "*Don Giovanni,*" or Werther in Goethe's novel "The Sorrows of Young Werther." I am sure this is because of the way in which my father was dominated by the two most important women in his life: his mother and his wife.

I remember waking up one morning and feeling sick. I had a headache and was hot all over and soon a rash appeared. The doctor was called and he announced that I had scarlet fever. Before the discovery of antibiotics, this was a dangerous disease. My brother was removed from the room we shared and my mother told me that he had been sent to live with family friends. I missed him and constantly asked for him. When I felt better and was allowed to get up, I opened the front door and saw two signs hanging on it. I was old enough to read a little, and on one of the signs I deciphered "scarlet fever" and on the other sign "diphtheria." A sign was obligatory when there was a patient with an infectious disease on the premises but here there were two. What could that mean? I knew that I did not have diphtheria, but when I asked my parents about the sign my question went unanswered. Eventually, Anna gave me the answer. While I was sick with scarlet fever, my brother was sick with diphtheria. He had not gone to stay with friends, but was lying in Anna's room. Because he was still sick, I was not allowed to see him. After what seemed an eternity, he recovered and we were reunited. I was happy, but before he could be moved back to our room, and Anna to hers, the rooms were fumigated. It was thought that fumigation would kill any remaining infectious germs: perhaps it did.

My parents arranged music lessons for my brother and me with two elderly spinsters who were recommended as music teachers by the Jewish school. Manfred was studying the piano and I the violin. I never became an accomplished violinist. I did not practice much, and my lessons lasted only two years; not enough time to provide a solid basis for the violin. Even so, I liked to play and I have always regretted that I did not go any further. Whenever my mother or father had a birthday, my brother and I would sneak early in the morning into the salon adjacent to their bedroom and "surprise" them with a serenade. We'd perform the one musical piece we played together—a simple folksong, then we each played a separate piece. When we were finished, the door between the salon and their bedroom would open and the parent whose birthday it was would appear to thank us for the "surprise."

The furniture in my parent's room—the bed, night tables and dressers—was made of very expensive mahogany wood. My parents explained that they had bought the furniture as an investment to safeguard their money during the period of steep inflation Germany went through in the 1920s. Money lost its value not daily, but hourly, and the simplest purchases (including bread) cost hundreds of thousands of marks.

I looked up to my brother. He was older and had privileges that I did not have. For example, there was the bicycle he had received as a birthday present. I had a hand-me-down child's bike that constantly broke down. I spent more time repairing it than riding it. He used his bike to attend various activities, such as to go to the sports field of the Jewish sports organization, *Maccabi,* to which we both belonged. I was envious and complained bitterly. A couple of years later he was given another new, shiny bike for *Hanukkah.* I was given a bike, too. It was the used one that he had just discarded. Now I was not only envious but resentful. As it turned out, his old bike was an excellent one. I rode it a lot and never had any trouble with it.

Manfred and I were never close as children. I cannot remember him playing with me, or talking with him about anything that seemed important. In Königsberg, we went to separate schools. Manfred attended the German *Gymnasium,* a high school oriented towards the classics, and I attended the Jewish school. We never talked about the differences in our experiences, never shared what was happening to us or how we felt about it. During our childhood we always remained apart.

Friends

On a warm summer day when I was four- or five-years-old, our nursemaid, *Fräulein* Martha, took me to a lake in the *Volksgarten* (the People's Garden). A little friend named Lore Thal came with us. *Fräulein* Martha undressed us to put on our bathing suits, and I looked at Lore. It was the first time I saw what little girls look like. I must have been impressed, since I remember the incident so well. As we grew up, we remained friends. Lore left for Holland a few weeks after Crystal Night in a children's transport that had been organized to save Jewish children from the Nazis. After that I never saw her again. Lore was the first child I can remember, and the first friend I ever had.

I didn't have any other friends until I started going to the Jewish school, where there were two boys I played with regularly. On the mornings when I went to school by way of the *Kaiserstrasse* rather than along the river, I passed by the home of Bernard Czernobilski, and we would walk together. When we went home after school, I'd frequently go up to his apartment for a snack and playtime, and sometimes he would visit me at our home. Erwin Petzall was my other close friend, but he lived further away in the new part of the town. To visit him, I had to take the streetcar. Ten blocks after it rumbled past the *Kaiser-Wilhelm-Platz* and the castle, I got off at the *Nordbahnhof,* the North Railway Station. The station was new, having been built in 1930, mostly for regional trains. A few years later it would be used for more sinister purposes. This was where the newer section of town began—it was modern, elegant and affluent. From the station I walked the few blocks to Erwin's house where his mother frequently had hot chocolate and cookies waiting for us. We spent a lot of time together playing and doing homework. Bernard and Erwin were my closest friends. In 1937, my parents sent me to a home for Jewish children near Berlin where I was to spend my summer vacation. Erwin was with me on the train, and we shared a room at the home. I was quite independent and glad to be away from home, but Erwin was homesick and frequently cried. At night I had to comfort him until he quieted down and went to sleep.

A girl named Henny Reif lived across from the factory office building, and we sometimes played together in her apartment, but she never came to our home although it was only a short walk away. My mother thought it was inappropriate for a girl to play at a boy's home, even though Anna was there to take care of us. We were seven-, eight-, nine- and finally ten-years-old. And then there was Judith Wolff, who I loved and who had "been won in the lottery" rather then being "delivered by the stork" like me. I wanted to invite her to my eighth birthday party, but my mother would not allow it, just as she refused to let Henny visit our house. It was improper to invite a girl to a boy's birthday party.

I played with my brother's older friends more often than I did with my own. They tolerated me when I tagged along with them. My brother invited them to spend *Silvester,* New Year's Eve, at our house, and I shared in their celebrations. As was customary, we melted lead in a spoon and threw it into a glass of water. The lead pieces solidified and the shapes were supposed to forecast our future. They all were wrong. None predicted what would lay soon lay ahead of us. Then at midnight, we followed another custom: we ate *Pfannkuchen* (jelly-filled doughnuts).

Summer Vacations

Shortly after my parents were married in 1924, they bought a summer house in Neuhäuser, a village near Königsberg. They still owned it when Manfred was born. My mother liked to spend the summer at the house, where my father would join her for weekends. But so many guests—invited and uninvited—came to stay that she found herself spending her entire time cooking and cleaning. Shortly after Manfred was born, the house was sold.

From then on, my parents liked to spend their vacations at a couple of sea-side resorts on the Baltic Sea near Königsberg. Their favorite resorts were in the fishing villages of Cranz and Rauschen. Manfred and I were taken along and left in the charge of our nursemaid. We'd set out for the *Nordbahnhof* to take the train. After an hour's train ride, we'd take a bus to the resort. I'd never been on a bus before. They were so much bigger than cars and I wondered how they could be parked and then driven so close to each other without touching.

Once we settled into our lodgings, I started the summer fun by visiting the villages. I delighted in all the little houses that lined the streets and were so different from the houses at home. They were only one or two stories high, and many of their roofs were covered with straw instead of shingles. Storks built nests on the roofs and I watched as they came and went bringing food to their babies. Fishermen hung their nets up to dry in front of their houses.

Cranz was the largest of these villages. It had a small boardwalk lined with restaurants and tourist hotels. But many tourists preferred to stay in smaller houses that had been converted to inns or even with the families of fishermen. There was a synagogue in Cranz that belonged to the Jewish community of Königsberg, though it was no longer in use. The economic restrictions imposed by the Nazis on the Jews caused the once thriving community to grow short of money. Because of that the synagogue was sold after it stood empty for a few years.

In the summer, Cranz and all these other quiet little villages came to life with the influx of the visitors from the nearby city. The beaches resounded with the noise we children made while we played on the sand or in the sea, while the adults relaxed and sought protection from the sun sitting on their beach chairs under big umbrellas.

I particularly remember the summer of 1934. My parents took lodgings at an inn. My room was just under the roof and up a narrow staircase. It was small and it had a window that overlooked the straw village roofs and their storks. Beyond the thatched roofs I could see fishing boats in the water, and would occasionally see the rising smoke that trailed after a large ship. In the evenings I could see the fishing boats on the beach next to their nets. Early in the morning, when I looked out the window, I'd see the boats heading out to sea with two or three men on board. In the afternoon they returned, full of still quivering fish. Being a fisherman was not without danger. Sudden storms threatened the little boats, and there were times when some men did not return at the end of the day. A few years later I saw the movie "Captains Courageous," which was about such fishermen. I thought of the men I'd seen, although the ships in the movie were much larger than the little boats of the resort villages. On those vacations, my father would spend the weekdays in the city and join us for the weekends.

We ate a lot of fish—cooked, smoked or fried. My favorite was smoked flounder. I have never since eaten smoked flounder as good as what was served in those resort villages on the Baltic. Fish was a staple that was made into soup, main dishes, sandwiches, snacks—freshly caught, freshly prepared, freshly eaten.

The days at the beach were spent under the ever-watchful eyes of *Fräulein* Martha. Since I had not yet learned to swim, I'd wade into the water close to the shore and collect amber, the yellow petrified resin found on the beaches of the Baltic Sea. I found many little pieces that the water had washed ashore. Sometimes, the amber enclosed a bit of a fossil plant or an insect. Larger pieces were valuable and made into jewelry, but the little pieces I found were for fun. I loved the jewel-like material. Some pieces looked like brilliant gold and others like dark copper. Even now I am fond of amber, and catch myself looking at displays of amber jewelry in store windows searching for the rare insects inside the stones that increase their beauty and their cost. For me, amber always brings back happy childhood memories.

In the afternoons, I'd run off to help the fishermen as they returned with their catch. On a good day their boats were filled with a variety of fish—large and small, but all colorful, alive and wiggling. I helped push and pull the boats onto the beach and helped to hang up the nets to dry, and sometimes helped unload the boats. I was not alone in doing so as there were plenty of other little boys and girls doing the same thing. The kind fishermen were friendly and tolerant, even though I'm certain we disturbed them while they worked. For me it was a great adventure. My ambition was to go out on a boat with the fishermen. One night I had a dream. I got up early, sneaked out of the inn and ran down to the beach hoping that a fisherman, maybe the one I helped the previous afternoon, would invite me to go out with him for the day. One of the fishermen recognized me, and said that, yes, I could go with him. I helped him put the empty nets in the boat and we started out to sea. The sky was blue, the water calm. After an hour, we spread the nets in the sea. When the nets were full, we pulled them in, emptied the catch into the boat, rowed to another spot and cast the nets overboard again. We repeated the same procedure a few times. When the sun stood high in the sky, the fisherman took his lunch and started to eat. My mouth was watering for the smoked flounder on his bread. I hadn't brought any lunch. But the fisherman rewarded me for my hard work by sharing his lunch with me. When the boat was full we started back to the shore. As we approached the beach I saw *Fräulein* Martha frantically waving her arms and running back and forth. She did not know where I was. When we got back, she didn't scold me for taking off without telling her where I was going, but instead wrapped me in her arms and gave me a long hug. She was so relieved. The other children who had joined the search cheered me. But alas, it was just a dream and I woke up under the thatched roof of the inn, having never left the shore.

In the first week of August of that year, i.e., 1934, I had already gone to bed and was alone in my room, when suddenly, the church bells started ringing, and they kept on ringing for several hours—until midnight. The next morning I was told that the ancient president of Germany, Paul von Hindenburg, had died. I was only six years old, but sensitized by what I experienced in the city, I feared that his death would only make matters worse. Hitler's deadly grip on Germany had tightened, sealing our fate.

Fräulein Martha left us in 1935, and we never returned to Cranz or Rauschen. From 1935 on, my parents sent my brother and me away for our vacations. For three consecutive summers, Manfred and I traveled to different places. In 1935 I was sent to a *Kinderheim* (a children's vacation home) in the *Riesengebirge* (the Mountains of the Giants), a mountain range near the Czech border. The *Kinderheim* was in Krumhuebel, a village at the foot of the *Schneekoppe*, a snowy mountain the name of which translates to "snow cap." The family pediatrician had planted a bug in my parent's ear: I had weak bronchia and he had said the mountain air would strengthen them. I don't know if it did my bronchia any good, but my parents could not have chosen a better place. I loved everything about the *Riesengebirge* mountains; the hikes, the view when the sun set in the evening, the panoramas when our hikes took us to higher altitudes. We hiked into nearby Czechoslovakia, through pine woods and fields covered with flowers, enjoying the smells of the soil and the plants. When we crossed the border there was nobody there to check, and we came back the same way. After that hike, I often thought about how easy it had been to cross the border, even though once I returned home, I once again listened to anxious discussions about visas that were needed to cross borders and how difficult it was to get them. But in the *Riesengebirge,* we simply walked across. I treasured that vacation and have loved the mountains ever since.

For my next vacation, in the summer of 1936, I was sent to Kolberg, a small town on the Baltic in the Pomerania region. Kolberg was known for its mineral baths. Once again I had been sent there on the recommendation of my pediatrician. Apparently, Krumhübel had not helped my bronchia enough and this year the bronchia required waters rich in minerals. As far as I could tell, nothing was wrong with my bronchia. I never felt sick, did not cough, did not have any pains and was as active as the other children. This time the *Kinderheim* was orthodox Jewish. My room was next to the owner's bedroom. Every morning I was awakened by a foul smell that seeped under the door from that room. The orthodox owner was forbidden by his beliefs to shave with a knife. Instead, he used an ill smelling chemical that had the odor of rotten eggs. I shared the room with a teenager, and sometimes he would creep into my bed early in the morning which woke me up. He wanted to play sexual games with his innocent little roommate. I did not know what he was up to because I knew nothing about sex. Nothing much happened and I did not complain. I didn't know any better.

Every morning I was taken to a bathhouse a few blocks away. I spent half-an-hour immersed in a tub full of warm water that smelled only a little better than the smell that woke me in the morning. I also was taken to the beach, but it was not much fun. There were no fishermen and no amber to search for. All I could do was play in the sand at the edge of the water, which I found boring. Kolberg was a real town and, with the other children, I went for walks in the town. On the day before I returned home, I bought a small box covered with sea shells and other gifts to take home as presents for my parents and my brother. I did that on an impulse. It was the first time I ever thought of taking presents home. This year, my parent's choice had been a poor one: I had not enjoyed the vacation.

The next year, 1937, my destination was Lehnitz, a home for Jewish children located near Berlin. This time it wasn't the pediatrician who had decided where

I was sent because there were other, weightier considerations. Lehnitz was one of the few remaining places in Germany where Jewish children could spend their summers. I was no longer welcome in non-Jewish camps or vacation homes. "*Juden nicht erwünscht*" reigned.

My friend Erwin Petzall and I took the train from our *Hauptbahnhof* to Berlin. It was an eight-hour ride followed by a shorter second ride to Lehnitz. After we left Königsberg, the train crossed the Polish Corridor that separated East Prussia from the rest of Germany. When we stopped at Dirschau, Polish police sealed the wagon doors from the outside, and the train proceeded through the Polish territory without stopping. On the western border, the German police in Schneidemühl removed the seals. The process was reversed on the return trip.

Lehnitz was situated among trees near a lake. We arrived in the late after-noon and were given a room together. After unpacking, we went down to a din-ing room crowded with children from all over the country. There were many more children at this camp than there had been in Kolberg or Krumhübel. Our activities started the next day. We went to the lake, we played games in the for-est or on the lawn surrounding the house and we went for walks. For the first time I was also given chores to do in the house. I helped set the tables before meals and cleaned up after them, and I did outdoor chores like picking weeds. I did not mind. At visiting day for parents, together with other children, I set the tables under the trees with cookies, juice and other snacks. My parents did not come. Königsberg was too far away. Instead, a cousin of my mother's, *Tante* Lehnchen, who lived in Berlin, came to visit.

I have made up a story about Lehnitz. Part of it is true, part false. There was a little girl there that same year by the name of Ursel Goldschmidt. True. I played with her and fell in love with her. False. Years later I fell in love with her for real and married her. True.

After Lehnitz one of my dreams came true. I spent a few days with *Tante* Lehnchen. She had promised to show me the city. For a long time I had wanted to know Berlin, and now I was given the opportunity. I was looking forward to this exciting end to my vacation.

I had the best time of my life with *Tante* Lehnchen. She spoiled me so much that I felt I was the most important person in the house. The apartment she lived in with her husband was located off the famous *Kurfürstendamm*, or the *Kudamm* as the Berliners called it. We went all over town, riding the *U-Bahn* (subway) and the elevated trains, all of which were new to me. We walked along a promenade called *Unter den Linden* (Under the Linden Trees), leading to the *Brandenburger*

Tor, a monumental gateway with five arches topped by an equally monumental chariot drawn by four horses. We visited the *Siegessäule,* the 210-foot Victory Column, topped by a twenty-seven-foot statue of Victory, which had been built after Germany's victorious war with France that ended in 1871. Then *Tante* Lehnchen took me to *Karstadt,* a department store that was part of a national chain. It seemed gigantic to my child's eyes; a paradise where anything the heart desired could be bought. Of course *Tante* Lehnchen bought me some toys, including a diver that looked like the ones I had seen in the river Pregel back home. We had a *Karstadt* in Königsberg, but compared to the one in Berlin, it was but a dwarf. I was a child from the provinces, overwhelmed by this showy, busy world of the capital.

The next two vacations, in 1938 and 1939, were my last in Germany, and they were quite different. I had spent the previous three summers in places designed for children. But now, Manfred and I spent several weeks with four other boys on an unusual farm called Lobitten. It was owned by an anti-Zionist Jew who made use of his farm to train young Jews to become farmers in Australia. It was similar to farms run by Zionist groups to prepare their members for life in *kibbutzim,* collective farm communities in Palestine. There were about thirty apprentice farmers, all young men. They raised pigs and cows and performed field work to produce a variety of crops. For me, to be on a farm was a great adventure.

Compared to the comfortable beds, clean bathrooms and dining rooms I had encountered during my previous three summers, Lobitten was a rough place. I slept in a bunk bed in a large room that was shared with the apprentices. At night, I covered myself with a scratchy woolen blanket, washed in the communal washroom, and used an outdoor outhouse located some distance away from the sleeping quarters. We ate our meals at wooden tables in the same room where we slept. The food was plain, but wholesome and very tasty. For breakfast there were big slices of black bread with marmalade that had been made on the farm. For lunch and dinner we ate meat and vegetable products that were also from the farm. The meat often came from a pig or a cow that I had seen alive only a few hours before. When the meat was pork, more often than not I had assisted in slaughtering the pig in the farmyard. I did that often and it did not bother me. This was why these animals had been raised. One of the apprentices taught me how to shoot a firearm. All in all we shared the lives of the young farmers, and nothing special was provided for us.

I took a small camera that my parents had given me for my birthday and followed the men around taking pictures as they performed their activities. I photographed the owner as he taught a class. I took pictures of the men at work in the fields. I went to the lake and photographed the ducks. I witnessed a calf being born and photographed it and its mother a few minutes later. Modesty was not writ large and one picture shows one of the men sitting in the outhouse, which I took when another man opened the door to occupy the seat next to him. There was no partition between the seats. Another picture I took shows a farm wagon returning from the fields, heavily loaded with crops, pulled by four sturdy farm horses as they entered the barn. On the roof of the barn was a stork's nest. As in Cranz and Rauschen a few years earlier, these birds built their nests on top of almost every barn. I still have most of these pictures, and they bring back happy memories.

We brought our bicycles and once in a while rode them to the beach which was only a few kilometers away. On the way, we had to pass through a village. In 1939 a large banner was put up on the road at the entrance of the village that said "*Juden nicht erwünscht*." We ignored it, although we were scared.

What I did not learn, even in the farm environment, was where babies came from. I saw calves and pigs being born, I saw the bulls mount the cows and I asked questions, but nobody volunteered the answers. I was ten years old in 1938 and eleven in 1939, a city boy on a farm where every child knew the facts of life through the simple observation of nature. But I had little contact with these children. I probably would have been too inhibited to ask them anyway; although I am sure that my brother at thirteen and fourteen knew all about it, he did not tell me. He considered me too little to know.

On the farm we were assigned tasks. I carried food out to the fields where the trainees worked. I helped in the barns with the hay and the cows, and I fed the pigs. I also had time to roam the farm without supervision. I rode the empty wagons to the fields, and sat on top of the crops as they returned with heavy loads. The farm yard was always bustling with activity. There was a smithy to shoe horses and repair tools. Farm implements, machines, wagons and tools were standing and lying around everywhere and each was unusual and interesting to me. I rode my bike out to the fields to lie down under a tree, watch the sky and daydream. It was so peaceful, so quiet, so different from what I was used to in the city.

I liked the farm. My time there was among the happiest of my childhood, so much so that I decided to become a farmer. However, later, when I had the opportunity, my mind had changed.

Kristallnacht

It was early in the morning, still dark. I was awakened by strange voices and steps in the hallway. Two men opened my bedroom door, looked into the dark room, closed the door and left. A little while later my father came in to bid me farewell and said that he did not know when he would return. This was strange. I did not understand what he meant. This was the night between the 9th and 10th of November, 1938. It is known as *Kristallnacht* or Crystal Night because of the many broken windows in Jewish-owned stores and apartments. In time, the event became known as the November Pogrom.

A few days earlier a member of the German Embassy in Paris, Ernst vom Rath, had been shot and wounded by a young Jew named Herschel Grynszpan, who was distraught over the deportation of his parents from Germany to Poland. I heard my parents express great concern over the shooting, and when the wounded man died, the concern rose to a fever pitch. "Something was bound to happen," they said. And what did happen was the "spontaneous" outburst of revenge planned and organized by the government. All over Germany, Nazi thugs invaded Jewish homes, businesses and houses of worship. They vandalized and destroyed whatever they could, set fire to synagogues and dragged men from their beds and sent them off concentration camps as a "punishment" for the "Jewish attack on Germany" that had been committed in the Paris shooting. Some cities were too far from the concentration camps for rapid transport. In those cities the men were jailed, which was what happened in Königsberg. My father was one of 450 Jewish men arrested and jailed on Crystal Night. Even in tiny Germau, with a remaining Jewish population of three—my aunt, uncle and cousin—the inhabitants took their revenge. My uncle and cousin were jailed. Fritz, the cousin, was only fourteen years old!

When I got up that morning, Mother was already dressed and pacing up and down the apartment. Normally, she was still asleep at that hour. She picked up the phone and put it down without talking. She opened and closed closets and drawers. She went to the windows and looked out, but I did not know what she was looking for. She told me that my father had been taken away by the *Gestapo*, the secret police, and that all of the city's Jewish men had been similarly picked up. The New Synagogue, where I went to school, had been set on fire and destroyed. The windows of Jewish residences had been broken, and the residences had been looted, vandalized and severely damaged. To confirm that, she did not have to go far. All she had to do was to look out the window at apartments across the street. The windows of Jewish-owned shops all over the city had also been broken and the shops themselves looted. Our apartment was one of the few to escape destruction. (Perhaps among the hordes of Nazis bent on destruction, violence and pillage, there were a few who were more compassionate, more reasonable and performed their assigned tasks in a relatively civil manner.) Mother was extremely anxious. She did not know what had become of my father or any of the other men.

I went out into the street and saw the damage. The Jewish apartments across from our house had been destroyed. Everywhere, there was glass on the sidewalk. Furniture had been broken, closets and drawers had been opened and ransacked and clothing and papers were left lying on floors. Much had been stolen, especially jewelry. Women and children just stood around with vacant expressions of incomprehension. They did not know what to do. I walked around the corner to the little synagogue on the side street. Its name was *Feuergasse* (Fire Lane), which was appropriate for what was happening that day. The interior had been totally destroyed, the benches overturned and the repository of the *Torah* scrolls was empty. I also walked to the orthodox synagogue, the Old Synagogue, next to the factory grounds. It was larger but the destruction and the empty *Torah* repository that I saw was much the same. Neither of these synagogues had been set on fire. The reason was that they were too tightly integrated into the neighborhoods, and thus too close to residential houses to be "safely" burned.

I was horrified by what I saw, but strangely, not surprised. This savage act of destruction and arrest was what the Nazis had threatened all along. This was what the "something" the adults had feared when Ernst vom Rath died. Crystal Night was the realization of the fear that had plagued me for so long. It was the acting out of the hatred heard in the Nazi songs as the Hitler Youth marched through the streets. It was the vengeance the "Stürmer" had portended, the fulfillment of the taunts the Nazi kids shouted and said they wanted to undertake when they attacked me on the streets. The new fear was, What would happen next?

Some Jewish men had been badly beaten. The director of the orphanage, who was also the assistant cantor of the synagogue and a friend of my parents, *Herr* Wollheim, had not only been beaten, but the Nazi hooligans who attacked him threatened to throw him in the Pregel alongside the street where the synagogue and the orphanage were located. The children in the orphanage had been awakened and driven out into the street in the middle of the night, dressed only in their pajamas. To the Nazi mind, even four-, five-, six-, seven-, eight- or nine-year-old children were guilty of the shooting in far off Paris. The death of vom Rath had to be avenged on them as well.

A few days after the pogrom, my mother came home and announced that she had learned where my father was. He was in the city jail with the other men arrested that day. There they were lodged together, fifteen to thirty men in each cell. Being in jail was a stroke of luck. They fared well compared to the thousands of others all over Germany who had been carted off to concentration camps. The reason the men were in the jail instead of being transported to concentration camps was that the closest camp was on the other side of the Polish Corridor. A transit fee had to be paid for the transportation of passengers through Polish territory, and the funds were not available. The men were treated courteously by their jailers and the women were allowed to take them food and blankets. Slowly, the men were gradually released to return to their destroyed homes. My father returned to our undamaged home.

One week after the pogrom, I saw the interior of the New Synagogue. The orphanage had been ransacked, but because the destruction there was less severe, it was pressed into service to do double duty as a school. The school principal and some of the older students had repaired the damage as best they could. The yard of the orphanage was adjacent to the yard of the synagogue. The two yards were separated by a fence that had some holes large enough for a child to squeeze through. I ducked through one of the holes and entered the synagogue by a back entrance. The damage was beyond my wildest imagination. The pews were broken and overturned. I could see the sky though the gaping holes in the roof. Everywhere there was soot, dust and dirt. As in the other synagogues, the *Torah* scrolls and their precious ornaments were gone. As I surveyed this horrible scene, I was aware of the irretrievable loss. Everything that I had loved and experienced in this building—the services, the choir, my visits to the organist high up above the altar, the school and its classrooms—were gone forever. All of that had gone up in flames. I went back to visit the ruins of the synagogue many times. For some inexplicable reason, I could not tear myself away. On one occasion, I found a small child's *Torah*—a printed one, not a real handwritten one—lying amid the rubble. It was dirty, but I took it with me and kept it as a memento. When I left the destroyed synagogue for the last time I thought of the statement my father had made when he came home from jail. He had said, "After this, things cannot become any worse." Unbelievably, his faith in Germany remained undiminished.

As I walked through the synagogue my feet and legs got wet. The floor was inundated with water used by the firemen to extinguish the flames. When the alarm had been given and the fire trucks arrived, the firemen had been prevented by the Storm Troopers from putting out the fire until they were satisfied that the building could never be used again. And it never was. The ruins presented a hazard to the surrounding houses and to people who walked by on the street. Eventually, the charred remains of the synagogue were torn down and the dome was dynamited. I had always thought of the building as permanent; something that would be there forever. I was wrong. The proud symbol of the proud Liberal Jewish community had lasted a mere forty-two years. I was shocked and saddened. Some weeks later, religious services for the entire Jewish community resumed in the Old Synagogue, which had been cleaned up and restored. The conflict between traditionalists and reformers that had lasted two centuries had been set aside. More pressing needs led to a closing of the ranks between the two previously antagonistic factions of the community.

After Crystal Night the debate about the future of the German Jews under National Socialism came to an end. With few exceptions, even the most patriotic and assimilated German Jews recognized that the end had come for them in Germany. But just then, when the need was greatest, most countries in the world closed their doors to Jews, making escape virtually impossible.

Crystal Night brought many changes to our family. From that point forward, family and business finances were controlled by a government imposed trustee. He released only the minimum funds the family needed to live on. These measures applied to all Jewish businesses, and were designed to enable the government to keep track of Jewish wealth. Henceforth, Jews were not allowed to own firearms. Miraculously, this edict lead to our salvation.

All Jews had to obtain a *Kennkarte* (identity card). One day our family went to the nearest police station to be issued the document. I was photographed so that my left ear showed on the picture. The shape of the ear was thought to be a unique identifier in addition to the fingerprints of my right and left index fingers. I signed the card as Siegfried Israel. Israel was the new second name that all Jewish males, adults and children alike, had to use. My father signed as Erich Israel and my brother as Manfred Israel. For similar reasons my mother was called Malwine Sara. The first of the four pages of the *Kennkarte,* which looked like a passport book, had a large "J" imprinted on them. It instantly identified its holder as a *Jude*, a Jew.

Some countries, most notably England and Holland, had offered to accept Jewish children in order to save them from the Nazi terror. Jewish communities all over Germany organized transports for children to be shipped out. My parents made preparations for me to leave on a transport to England, but did not tell me. A couple of weeks after Crystal Night, I came home to find my cousin Fritz sitting in my room. He had just arrived from Germau after having been released from jail. He had been threatened with incarceration in a concentration camp if he did not leave Germany within a few weeks. When my parents returned later that day, they told me of their plan to send me to England. But before I could express my shock, they said that they had given my place on the transport to Fritz to save him from the concentration camp. So Fritz went to England instead of me. We gave him an emotional farewell during which he gave me a wet kiss on my cheek, wet because he was crying, and so was I.

Seven weeks after *Kristallnacht*, in late 1939, my parents got my brother and me up early one morning and took us to the railway station. We were put on a train bound for Hamburg. They thought that life was becoming too dangerous for us in Königsberg due to the increasingly violent anti-Semitic incidents that had become commonplace. Family friends in Hamburg had offered to take us in. Hamburg was Germany's major port and most cosmopolitan city. It had always been influenced by the foreigners who passed in and out of the city. There was little Nazi violence and few party marches. We had to change trains in Berlin, and we entered the waiting room of the station after eight hours on the train. We were hungry and wanted something to eat. When we entered, we had overlooked the ubiquitous sign telling us to keep out, and before we had the chance to buy anything a man kicked us out. I was neither surprised nor offended. I had come to expect such treatment.

Hamburg

We arrived in Hamburg hungry and tired. We settled in with the Aarons, the family that had offered to care for us. Mr. and Mrs. Aaron were a little younger than my parents. They had no children, but three nephews lived with them in their large apartment on the top floor of a five-story building. An ancient elevator provided transportation up and down. It was slow and often in need of repair, so that I frequently climbed the stairs to the apartment. The apartment was large enough to accommodate the couple, the nephews and us. It had a balcony that overlooked a large park adjacent to the quiet residential neighborhood. We shared a room with one of the nephews, who was eighteen years old.

Shortly after our arrival, I started going to a Jewish school for boys, *Talmud-Torah*, a name traditionally given to a religious school. In spite of its name, the school provided a normal, academically oriented high school education. The walk from the apartment to the school took about twenty minutes. On the way, nobody taunted me, nobody threw stones at me and there were no ugly incidents. After Königsberg, Hamburg seemed like a different world. I was in the 5th grade. In high school this was called "*Sexta*," and every subsequent grade had a similar Latin name, which counted down from this initial 5th grade: *Quinta, Quarta, lower Tertia, upper Tertia,* and so on, for a total of eight years. I made new friends, but none of them acquired the importance in my life as my friends from Königsberg. The school building had proper classrooms, a schoolyard for breaks and a formal entrance portal, all of which was quite different from the makeshift informality of my previous school. Next to the school was a synagogue that looked similar to Königsberg's New Synagogue. It had also been damaged on Crystal Night and was now closed. I never saw the inside. After I left Hamburg, it too was torn down.

From the Aaron's house I often took the streetcar to the city center, located on the Alster River. Elegant cafes overlooking the river opened their doors to tourists and natives alike, but not to us. As elsewhere in Germany, there were the ubiquitous *"Juden nicht erwünscht"* signs. Large office buildings and stores faced the Alster across a wide boulevard, called *Jungfernstieg,* Virgin's Path. I was impressed by the elevators inside these buildings that had the strange name of *Pater Noster.* An unending chain of cabins without doors moved from the bottom to the top on one side, and then back down on the opposite side in an unending circular motion. They never stopped and passengers entered and left the cars while they were in motion. The first time I went into one of these cabins and went all the way up to where the motion changed from up to down right under the roof, I was scared. I was afraid that the cabins would turn upside down, that the ceiling would become the floor, and I would then myself be turned upside down and fall. Of course this did not happen. But what was most impressive was the massive 19th century Renaissance style town hall. Dark and brooding, it was several stories high, a city block long and had an enormous swastika flag flying in front of it on a separate flagpole. To me, the town hall was the symbol of this great city, as the castle had been for Königsberg. Another of Hamburg's attractions was a world famous zoo and circus, the *Hagenbeck,* which was off limits to us.

Close by was the Elbe River with Germany's largest port. There were gigantic freight and passenger ships, huge cranes and smaller boats all coming and going in what seemed to be perpetual motion. To get to the port, I had to walk through a busy tunnel beneath an arm of the river that led from the city to the docks. It was used by cars, horse carts, trucks and pedestrians. On the other side was a pedestrian boardwalk that offered a perfect view of the port. After witnessing the activity in Hamburg, Königsberg's port seemed like a little village backwater.

Next to the port was the neighborhood of St. Pauli, which included the notorious *Reeperbahn.* I heard people talking about it in hushed voices, even at the Aaron's. I did not understand what it was, and nobody told me when I asked. In fact, it was the largest center of prostitution in all of Europe, augmented by bars and nightclubs—anything that a sailor, a tourist or an adventurous resident might desire.

I was a faithful customer at several of the small commercial establishments in our neighborhood. I patronized the drug store, the bakery, the post office and the savings bank where I kept my savings of five marks.

It was in Hamburg, at age eleven, that I finally received my first sex education from the teenager with whom we shared our room. He liked little boys and provided his information at a price: his pupil was required to play sexual games with the teacher. I forever wondered whether my brother had also been solicited, and if so, what his reply was. I never asked him and never found out. We were not close enough for that kind of conversation. In hindsight, the teenage boy's treatment of me was a case of what later became known as child molestation—a consequence of those stork and lottery stories parents told their children.

I returned to Königsberg for summer vacation. It was my last visit to the city, and a number of surprises awaited me. The first was that when I arrived home, our apartment was full of strange people. My parents economic circumstances were such that they had been forced to rent out rooms. The trustee did not provide them with enough money to cover their expenses. But there was also a more sinister reason. A new regulation allowed owners of apartment buildings to cancel the leases of Jewish tenants, and Jewish families were forced out of their houses. The authorities concentrated them in so-called (Jew's Houses), mostly in our neighborhood in the old part of town. Sometimes it was possible to retain one's apartment by taking in renters. So my parents had rented their bedroom and living rooms to a widow with two teenage daughters and a son and then were able to continue to live in their own apartment. Prior to my arrival, my parents had said nothing to me about this turn of events.

My next surprise came when I visited the factory. I went there right after I arrived, and I saw only strange workers. *Frau* Marwilski was not there, nor was anybody else I knew. I was told that the factory no longer belonged to my parents and that I had to leave. The request was friendly, but firm. My parents had mentioned nothing about this either. The world I had known had collapsed. The Nazi authorities had forced my parents to sell—no, to give—the business to a Nazi-appointed "buyer." Regardless of the money that changed hands, my parents received no benefit from the sale because the proceeds went to the trustee to be incorporated with the other family assets. "Home" had become a strange, unfamiliar place.

A few days after our arrival in Königsberg, my brother and I left for our second and final vacation in Lobitten. Not much had changed since the previous year, and only the *"Juden nicht erwünscht"* sign at the entrance of the village we had to cross to get to the beach was new. After the vacation at Lobitten, we returned to Hamburg and I never again saw Königsberg.

One day, back in Hamburg, a letter arrived from my parents. It mentioned the possibility of emigrating to Chile. Nothing can describe the joy and the relief I felt upon receiving this news. My parents had finally acted and we were going to escape. I remembered the discussion my parents had had only fifteen months earlier when my mother had exclaimed, "Chile? That earthquake country? Never!" But now, after the Crystal Night, her objections vanished. Earthquakes or not, Chile had become the haven we so desperately needed. It was even more desperately needed because of an event that had occurred in Königsberg, which I was not aware of at the time, but was the reason my parents had decided to act.

In Hamburg, my brother and I started taking Spanish lessons. Twice a week we went to the house of a teacher and dutifully learned a few new words: *la mesa* (the table); *la casa* (the house); *yo tengo, tu tienes, el tiene* (I have, you have, he has). I lost interest in school, after all, I would soon be gone. Shortly thereafter my parents came to Hamburg, and together we went to Bremen to pick up our visas at the Chilean consulate.

Prior to departing Königsberg, my parents packed two large wooden container boxes, or *Lifts*, with furniture, clothing, and the industrial sewing machines they hoped to use in Chile to earn a living. Packing a *Lift* was no simple matter. An application had to be made to the police that included a list identifying each item packed with the date it had been acquired. This had to be done down to the last pair of socks. Any new purchases were forbidden to be taken out of the country. The intent was to prevent emigrants from using their money to purchase things that could later be sold in the country of destination. The emigrant's money had to be left behind in Germany, where it was confiscated by the government. On the appointed day, the police sent agents to supervise the packing of the *Lifts* to make sure that nothing was packed that was forbidden, such as jewelry or money. My parents' *Lift* application list was eight pages long. Here are some of the items included in the list:

- a blue suit, acquired in 1931
- a pair of pants, ditto
- a raincoat, repaired

- a bathrobe, damaged
- 4 covers for heating pads, wedding presents, 1924
- 1 piano, ditto
- 3 pictures, ditto
- 7 pillows, ditto
- 7 coffee cups, gifts
- 1 briefcase, acquired in 1931
- 1 hot water bottle, acquired at wedding, 1924

And so on. The banality of the bureaucratic requirement to produce such a list defies imagination. However, my parents succeeded in smuggling some forbidden jewelry into their *Lifts*. The jewelry had been sewn into the seams of their clothing. The *Lifts* were shipped to Holland, and from there they were to be forwarded to Chile. However, they never arrived. Either they were destroyed during the bombing of Rotterdam or pilfered while in storage.

On September 1, 1939, I left the apartment to go to school. A big crowd had gathered around a loudspeaker at the gas station across from the apartment building. I joined the crowd and heard Hitler's voice proclaiming that the Nazi Army had successfully crossed the border into Poland to punish the Poles for their attacks on German citizens. In fact, the alleged attacks had been organized and staged by the Germans themselves. The German invasion of Poland marked the onset of World War II. The next few days I anxiously read the newspaper headlines that reported British and French ultimatums, followed by their declarations of war. Suddenly, it appeared that there would now be no emigration to Chile. I felt trapped. My highest hope had come to nothing.

I closed my savings account and prepared for war. How? I spent my savings on batteries for my flashlight because a blackout had been decreed throughout Germany. Rationing was introduced. When I was sent to the bakery I had to take the rationing book in addition to money. From the rationing book the baker extracted little coupons, one coupon for every 100 grams of bread. When the coupons were gone, no more bread could be purchased. The procedure was the same at the butcher shop. The food we ate was carefully measured to insure that it would last until the next rations were available. Air raid sirens sounded almost every night, and I'd get up with the rest of the family to stand on the balcony and watch for the "enemy" planes that never came.

In the middle of October, with the war six weeks old, the unexpected happened: Manfred and I were told to meet our parents in Berlin so that we could join them on the voyage to Chile. We packed our belongings, said good bye to the Aarons, whom we never saw again, and left. Much of Hamburg would not survive the war. The center of the town, the port facilities and the adjacent old city would all be targeted by Allied bombers in their raids over Germany.

Escape

Our escape was nothing less than miraculous. My parents told me the story. The factory's chief clerk, the Nazi Meyer, had, unbeknownst to my parents, embezzled a large amount of money from the firm, and he wanted his employer out of the way so that the theft would not be detected. His opportunity came with *Kristallnacht* and the edict that Jews were forbidden to own firearms. One day in the summer of 1939, *Herr* Meyer opened the office safe in the presence of my father and some other witnesses. Oh, what a surprise! There was a revolver in the safe! *Herr* Meyer charged his boss, my father, with a violation of the law. He told my father that much to his regret he was obligated to call the *Gestapo*. This, of course, meant immediate incarceration in a concentration camp. The *Gestapo* cited my father to a "hearing" two days later at their headquarters.

At the hearing, the *Gestapo* officer in charge revealed himself to be a decent individual. He probably suspected that the gun had been a planted by *Herr* Meyer, and instead of immediately arresting my father, he allowed him two months to arrange for his emigration. Failing that, my father was told he would be sent to a concentration camp. My father presented his case to the Jewish community and appealed for assistance. Because my parents were well respected, both for their past monetary contributions and for their participation in the community's philanthropic activities, the community agreed to help. The Chilean visas and the tickets for an Italian ship that would take us to Chile were arranged.

Herr Meyer's plot to destroy my father was transformed into our salvation. We still had extended family and many family friends living in Königsberg at that time, but we were the last to leave. All of those left behind were murdered.

Taps

In October of 1938, there were 2,086 Jews in Königsberg. A Nazi publication stated that as of February 1938, there remained 201 Jewish businessmen, thirty-eight doctors and twenty-two lawyers, but the publication was mute on their ability to function in their professions. By May 1939, 500 more Jews had left the city. Some had emigrated, and others had moved to other cities in Germany, such as Berlin. Beginning in 1939, some Jews had been forced to move from their residences to be concentrated in *Judenhäuser*. By 1940, the program was intensified and extended to all Jews that remained in their houses or apartments. They were allocated one room per family, regardless of family size. On September 1, 1941, Jews were forced to wear the yellow star.

The final destruction of the Jewish community began in the summer of 1942, when the deportations began. Michael Wieck[8] writes that deportations started with small groups sent directly to death camps, while older people were initially sent to Terezin (Theresienstadt), from which they were subsequently deported to the death camps in Poland. Some Jews committed suicide rather than face deportation. The non-Jewish population reacted with indifference. The property of the deported was swiftly appropriated, as the deported Jews were deprived both of their citizenship and their belongings.

Mass deportations were carried out in 1942 and 1943. Most of the transport trains left from the *Nordbahnhof* rather than the *Hauptbahnhof*, the main railroad station. The day came when a large transport of many hundreds of Jews was organized. Michael Wieck[9] describes how he, a half-Jew not yet subject to deportation, accompanied the deportees to the train that was to carry them to their fate. In his book he provides the names of many of the deportees on the train who were his friends and teachers. The teachers were also my teachers, and many of his friends were also my friends, among them Ruth Marwilski and Erwin Petzall. To this day, the destination of that particular train remains unknown because no one survived to tell the tale. Eventually almost all Jews were deported, and the 250-year-old Jewish community ceased to exist in 1943. It is estimated that between 1,000 and 1,500 Jews from Königsberg lost their lives. The total is uncertain because an unknown number of them were deported from other German cities or were caught in neighboring countries, such as Holland, after they had emigrated.

Sixty "privileged" Jews remained in Königsberg after the deportations. This was approximately the same number that had lived there in the year 1700. They were primarily living in mixed marriages or were the children of such marriages. Not all of them lived to see the end of the war.

The city did not survive the loss of the Jewish community for very long. The death of Königsberg commenced in August 1944, when Allied bombing raids ignited great fire storms that destroyed the inner city with its harbor, the commercial center, the castle, the 14th century cathedral and the residential districts where the inhabitants were burned to death in their houses. Over fifty percent of

---

[8] Michael Wieck, "Zeugnis vom Untergang Königsbergs—Ein Geltungsjude berichtet," Heidelberger Verlagsanstalt und Druckerei GMBH, 1990.

[9] Ibid.

the buildings were destroyed, and more than 3,500 people were killed in the Allied raids. Another 150,000 lost their homes. Fires burned for days before they could be extinguished.

In 1945, the advancing Red Army shelled Königsberg in a massive bombardment prior to entering the city in April 1945. The end came on the 9th of April, when the German Army capitulated. Sometime later, Soviet troops set fire to the buildings that had survived and the destruction was complete. Königsberg was dead. The *Götterdämmerung* that had begun on that infamous *Kristallnacht* in 1938 had come full circle: Valhalla had gone up in flames.

Before the war, 300,000 people lived in the city. At the end of the war, it is estimated that there remained 110,000, including military personnel. By 1947, once the military personnel had been removed as war prisoners and many of the remaining inhabitants died of hunger, disease and maltreatment by the Russian occupiers, there remained only 25,000 Germans. The city, together with the northern part of the province, was annexed by the Soviet Union and incorporated into the USSR. Ultimately, the surviving Germans were exiled and deported to East Germany. A few managed to reach the West, including Michael Wieck, who was one of the last two Jews in Königsberg. The other was his mother. Not a single German remained and the city was resettled by inhabitants from the Soviet Union. Dead Königsberg had been reborn as Kaliningrad, inhabited by Soviets, and rebuilt on the model of many other Soviet cities.

Few of Königsberg's former buildings remain today. The two railroad stations and the post office survived. So did the stock exchange, which was converted into a sailor's club. Surprisingly, the monument to the philosopher Immanuel Kant survived, next to the burnt-out cathedral, the Dom. Also still standing in 1993 was the Jewish orphanage that my school had moved to after *Kristallnacht*. It stood all by itself, the adjacent synagogue long since torn down, and no other buildings in sight.

Former inhabitants visiting the city reported that nothing was left to remind them of the past. Pictures and films confirm that judgment. Königsberg is dead, never to be revived. It was replaced by a new city, bearing no similarity whatever to what had been there before.

Who Survived?...

Cousins Herbert and Lola Blum, the children of *Tante* Friedel, after whom I was named, escaped to Palestine. I met Herbert again in Israel, but Lola died young and I never saw her again.

Cousins Curt and Martin Radzewski, sons of *Tante* Jenny, the oldest sister of my mother, escaped to Argentina. I met them there a few years later. Their half brother Fritz Freitag took my place on the children's transport to England. The British Government considered the teenager Fritz a potential enemy alien and deported him to Australia. Isolated there, he cut off all contacts with his relatives. I have not seen him again.

Tante Ella, the other sister of my mother, whose family spent Passover with us in 1935, left for Palestine right after their visit. The whole family survived in Israel.

My friends Bernard Czernobilski and Judith Wolff also escaped to Palestine. After the war I met Bernard in Israel and Judith in Zürich, Switzerland, where she was living at the time. We renewed our friendship, although neither of them remembered me.

Franz Kaelter, the principal of the Jewish school, escaped to Palestine together with one of the male teachers named Nussbaum.

Rudolf Pik, the cantor with the lovely voice, escaped to England together with his family shortly before the war broke out. Like cousin Fritz, the British considered him an enemy alien. He was interned and forced to do agricultural labor. After the war, the whole family went to Israel where he resumed for a time his career as an opera singer.

That is all.

...and Who Didn't?

Tante Jenny and her husband Willie Freitag were deported from Königsberg to the Theresienstadt (Terezin) concentration camp. Uncle Willie died there. Aunt Jenny was murdered in Auschwitz. Their daughter Eva, my oldest cousin, was deported with the 28th Transport leaving Berlin on the 2nd of March 1943. At the age of thirty, she was taken to Auschwitz where she was murdered.

Erwin Petzall and Henny Reif were deported from Königsberg. *Frau* Marwilski and her daughter Ruth were deported at the same time. Also deported at that time were the remaining teachers of the Jewish school, one man and three women. Among them was my mother's best friend *Tante* Kaete. They were murdered, but it is not known where.

Lore Thal was sent to Holland on a children's transport. She was taken in by a Dutch family. Survivors of that same transport have said that after the Germans invaded Holland, the host family became afraid and abandoned or betrayed her. She was caught by the invading Nazis, deported, and murdered. The location of her death remains unknown.

The Aarons, husband and wife, were deported from Hamburg. Their destination(s) and the place(s) of their murders are unknown.

Rabbi Reinhold Lewin, he who could not reconcile Zionism with being a German, was deported together with his wife and two children. All of them were murdered.

Almost all the children who remained in the school after I left were murdered.

Final Thoughts

To have escaped the German gas chambers and bullets counts as the greatest blessing of my life. I should be forever grateful to *Herr* Meyer for putting that gun in my father's office safe. Without it, my parents would never have acted and we, our whole family, would have been murdered too.

The latest research[10] shows that the deportation train that carried my friends from Königsberg probably went to Riga. Immediately upon their arrival, all of the deportees were shot. My relatives, *Tante* Jenny and Eva were gassed in Auschwitz. My thoughts stop when I try to think about their last hours and minutes. I simply cannot imagine what they experienced.

I cannot comprehend how a reputedly cultured people like the Germans could have designed and operated death factories as an industry. I cannot imagine how educated people—scientists and engineers—designed those machines, how workers installed and maintained them and how those operating the death trains went about their work with the full knowledge of the fate that awaited the passengers. No lectures, no books, no research papers have enlightened me. I doubt that any ever will. The holocaust will forever remain beyond my comprehension.

Postscript: Letters

A few letters survive that were written to my parents from those left behind. They date from late 1939 to the middle of 1941. They provide poignant testimony to the desperation that had set in by 1941 when all communication between those who remained behind and those who escaped ceased.

From the Aaron family in Hamburg there are two letters. The first is dated November 1939, and in it they ask whether they should bring their furniture when they emigrate, or whether they should buy new furniture abroad. The second letter, written only ten months later, expresses all loss of hope for emigration

---

[10] Schüler-Springorum, "Die jüdische Minderheit in Königsberg/Preussen 1871–1945," Vandenhoeck & Ruprecht, 1996.

and speaks of grueling poverty. They are no longer able to afford the price of postage stamps, let alone undertake new efforts at emigration.

There are also two letters from the Marwilskis, mother and daughter. The first is dated December 12, 1939, the second April 28, 1940. In addition to giving news of friends and acquaintances, they express a deep and abiding belief in God, thanking Him for the salvation of the Flatow family and invoking His protection for themselves. Ruth adds a "thousand kisses" and asks me to write to her. In the second letter she sends me birthday wishes. Later she became the girlfriend of Michael Wieck, who wrote the book about the destruction of the Jewish community and the city,[11] in which he described the deportation of Ruth and her mother with so many other friends and relatives. I never did write to Ruth. My regret for that omission, after rereading her letters more than fifty years after they were written, cuts deep.

Tante Kaete writes twice. Her first letter, dated September 1940, is in reply to a letter that I had written her earlier in the year. In reply, she says that my letter was read to the remaining students at the school, as were other letters from those who had left. She adds that the children took a particular interest in the letter from their "darling Schieps." In the second letter (May 1941) she reports that she has lost her teaching job because the school no longer has the money to pay all the teachers, and the other teachers are more in need of a job than she. Seventy students remain and they are combined into two classes. She plans to give private lessons to earn her living, but may have to share the single room in which she lives with another woman. That would make teaching there impossible. She said she remembers my brother and me, and she reports that my friends Erwin Petzall and Henny Reif are now in the upper class. She has absolutely no hope for emigration. And she adds, "In the meantime, my life and my old age draw to a lonely and wretched conclusion."

There is also a surviving telegram from "*Onkel* Willie," the husband of Mother's sister Jenny and cousin Fritz's father. He asks if there is any possibility to come to Chile, and if not, to Argentina or Bolivia. The date is February 1940. This is the last communication from that family.

What all these letters have in common is their complete hopelessness. The writers did not know about the holocaust yet. The "final solution" had not begun, but the dread and fear are present in every communication. Today we know that their fears proved prophetic. All who wrote these letters were murdered.

---

[11] Michael Wieck, op. cit.

Deutschland, Deutschland...

My father, as a medic
during World War I

My father, Erich
Flatow, ca. 1939

My mother, Malwine
Flatow, 1947

My brother
Manfred and I,
1932

My first day of
school, 1934

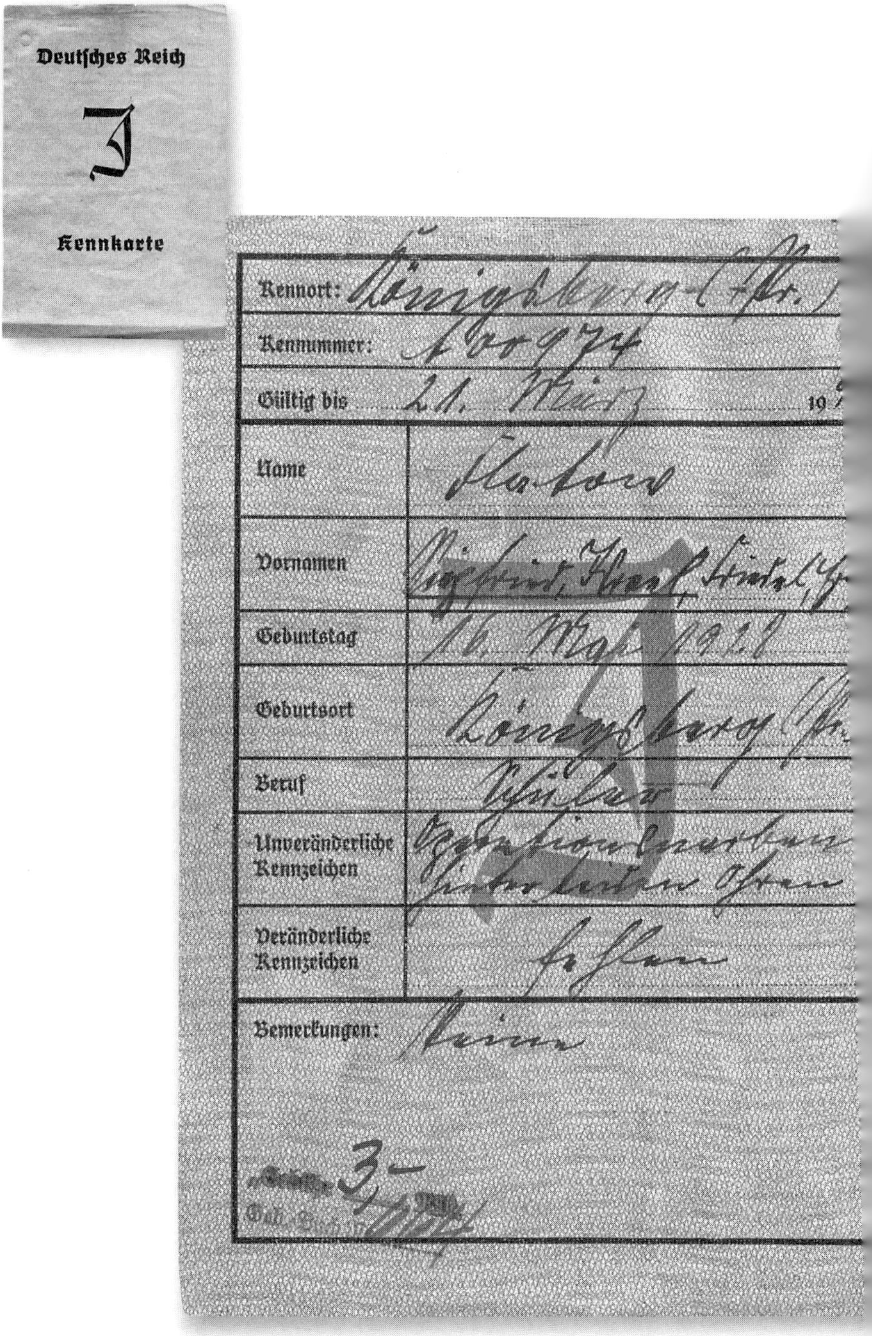
Deutsches Reich

J

Kennkarte

Kennort:	
Kennummer:	
Gültig bis	19
Name	
Vornamen	
Geburtstag	
Geburtsort	
Beruf	
Unveränderliche Kennzeichen	
Veränderliche Kennzeichen	
Bemerkungen:	

Kennkarte (identity card)

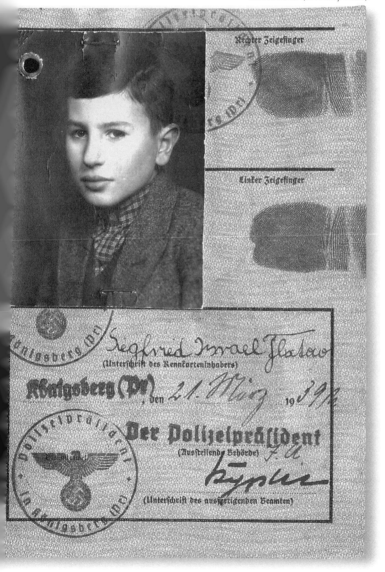

Our synagogue, outside...

...and inside

The castle

The river Pregel with the
castle in the background

Another view of the
Pregel with the century-old
warehouses

Moving a load into a warehouse

Market day

Selling fresh fish on market day

Vorstädtische Langgasse. In this block were
located the offices of my parents' factory.

The Schlossteich, the Castle
Lake. Here I went to ice
skate in wintertime.

Fishing boats in Cranz

Interlude: Good-bye, Europe

Conte Grande, the ship that
in 1939 brought us from
Genoa in Italy to Chile, in a
journey of four weeks

Puro Chile...

The statue of the Virgin on the
San Cristóbal, photo by author

Christ of the Redemption. Border
between Argentina and Chile at a
height of 12,800 ft., destination of
one of our hikes, photo by author

The view from my "study rock" on the Cerro Santa Lucía. The building in front is the Catholic University.

Mother attending to one of the outside seamstresses of the factory, ca. 1948

Ursel and I, 1948, on a hike
to the Abanico mountain

Ursel and I, 1948

Our (only) wedding picture,
19 December 1948

America, America...

Our first view of New
York: lower Manhattan,
photo by author

The Statue of
Liberty waved
her "welcome"
to us, photo by
author

A Maltese Interlude

King's Gate, main entrance to Valetta,
photo by author

Street in Valetta, photo by
author

Valetta's Grand Harbor

Maltese woman dressed in faldetta,
photo by author

Valetta waterfront, photo by
author

Typical village church (Zabbar); clocks on the
two towers show different times, photo by
author

At work in the Navy shop

America, America...

Our family in 1993, at
Steven's wedding, from left
to right: Ruth, myself, Ursel,
Steven, Daniel

The Shapiro
family in 1997;
clockwise from the
left: Tamara, Phil,
Elisa, Ruth, Laura

Steven and Nancy, 1993, at
their wedding

Robbie and James, 1998

Ursel and I in 1993 at
Steven's wedding

Ursel and I on a hike in
Germany (1994)

Interlude:
Good-bye, Europe

I STOOD ON THE DECK OF THE BIG SHIP, DOCKED IN THE PORT OF GENOA IN ITALY. The time was October 1939. The war in Europe was 6 weeks old. As the ship, called *Conte Grande,* departed, I sang the old German song "*Nun ade du mein lieb Heimatland*" (Farewell to you, my dear Homeland), only I substituted Europe for *Heimat,* giving the song the broader meaning as I had come to think of it. I did not yet know to what we owed our sudden escape, but no matter, we had escaped. I thought that this was a final farewell to Europe, a six-week journey with no return.

I was very much aware of our lucky, last minute escape, and could not contain my feelings of relief to have left Germany behind; left behind the hate, the daily threats, the indignities and the unprovoked attacks. I could now begin to shed my fears. My nightmares would not return to disturb my sleep. I understood the meaning of this emigration: we were traveling to a far-off, unknown land called Chile.

Our trip to Italy had been hectic. Italy still offered an escape route because it had not yet joined the war on the side of it's ally, Germany. Technically it was still neutral. After our hurried departure from Hamburg, Manfred and I met our parents in Berlin. When we arrived in the evening Berlin was dark, the blackout a precaution against Allied air raids that never came. The next day we went to the *Karstadt* department store for some last minute shopping and then boarded a train to Munich on our way to Genoa. We stopped in Munich long enough for me to visit a doctor to take care of a badly swollen and infected finger that had plagued me ever since I left Hamburg. Once the painful procedure was completed, we resumed our trip to Genoa. We shared the compartment with other emigrants, adults and children, who, just like us, were bound for Genoa and the *Conte Grande.* From the conversations among the adults, I got a sense of the tension and uncertainty about what might happen at the German-Italian border.

Would we be prevented at the last minute from continuing our journey and all be sent back into the hell we had just left? But their fears were groundless, all had gone smoothly. The border police had entered our compartment, politely asked for our passports, returned them without any comment, saluted and left. We arrived safely in Genoa.

My father had done something very clever just before the border crossing. Jews were allowed to take only token amounts of money with them when leaving Germany. I believe it was ten marks per person, the equivalent of about ten dollars for the four of us. My father carried an amount in excess of what was allowed. Just before the border crossing he had gone to one of the train's toilets and hidden that excess amount in a dry spot of the toilet tank. After the crossing he returned to retrieve the hidden treasure. It was not much, but it was enough to pay for a dingy little hotel room without a bath or hot water where we spent the night in Genoa, and later to allow us to buy a few small things along the way, on the ship and in the various ports where we stopped.

The next morning before the ship left, one of our two steamer trunks, which contained half of the belongings we were taking with us into exile, was missing. My father and I went frantically searched for it and finally found it on the dock some distance away from the ship. Perhaps people working for the transport company that brought it to the dock left it there so that they could steal it once the ship departed.

It was not until after the ship sailed from the harbor that I descended several stairs to take a first look at our third-class cabin. When I opened the door, I was confronted with a tiny room with two double bunk beds, one next to each wall, and a sink between them at the wall opposite the door. We fit our suitcases under the two beds, there was no other room for them. The four of us were to share that little space for the next six weeks. When a little later I went to the toilet located in the passageway in front of the cabin, I found several people already waiting for it. The same thing happened when I got up in the morning to take a shower. One toilet and one shower served eight cabins, about twenty-five to thirty people in all.

Three times a day I went up to the dining room to eat. I sat at a long table with twenty other people. There was no privacy, but on the other hand this arrangement had an important advantage. While we ate our pasta with a little meat, very little meat, followed by a dried-out pastry, we could exchange the latest news, discuss the most recent events and worry about the uncertain future that faced all of us around that table. Many times when the weather was rough, I donated this indifferent food to the sea as soon as I had eaten it. I'd run outside, stand at the ship's rail and share it with the fish. Other passengers up and down the rail did likewise. But what did all that matter compared to the feeling of safety I experienced anew every day? Even so, at that moment our safety was not complete. Dangers lurked from another quarter. Crew and passengers alike were afraid of wartime attacks by French or British airplanes or submarines. The sides of the ship where painted with large Italian flags. A huge flag was displayed, lying flat on the rear deck for overflying aircraft to see. It was illuminated by bright lights every night. The flag was not removed until we passed Gibraltar and were well out into the Atlantic.

The difficult third-class conditions created many tensions between the passengers, sometimes resulting in harsh words being exchanged. In the cabin across from us lived a Jewish woman from Vienna who had converted to Christianity. Her hair was dyed blond and she looked to be in her forties. She wanted nothing to do with her former co-religionists. She felt herself superior and I heard her proclaim this in a loud voice again and again, in front of our cabin, on deck and in the dining room. Standing in line for the bathroom or shower, she sometimes attempted to push ahead because of her not being Jewish. It was grotesque, more so because she was on this ship for the same reasons we were. The Nazis had considered her a Jew, no different from the rest of us who had not converted. The other passengers in our small section, all Jewish, soon tried to put her in her place with some well chosen words pointing out our common fate. But although she no longer tried to push ahead, she did not shut up during the whole trip.

Our accommodations, however, were paradise compared to the steerage conditions of hundreds of Spanish Civil War refugees who came on board in Barcelona. When I looked into a cargo hold converted to receive these unfortunate victims of the war, I saw the rows upon rows of bunk beds set up for them. From where I stood I could not see where they washed, what toilets they used or where they ate. I never tried to find out because I was too young to be curious about their fates. The passengers of the various classes, from first-class to steerage, never mixed with each other and in any event, there was an insurmountable language barrier between me and these Spanish refugees. I had not progressed beyond the lessons in Hamburg that had taught me "*la mesa; la casa; yo tengo, tu tienes, el tiene.*"

Like other passengers, we disembarked in Barcelona for a visit of the town, which had been severely damaged by the civil war. Nevertheless, the city with its wide, tree lined streets caused a deep impression on me that I never forgot. When years later I returned for a brief visit, I could still pick out some of the landmarks. It was our last city in Europe, a final farewell.

At one time during the trip there was a rare breach in the separation of the classes; a young Jewish refugee traveling by himself in first-class invited me to lunch at his table. We met at one of the stopovers when the passengers left the ship and mingled. In the first-class dining room, we sat on comfortable chairs at a small table covered with a white table cloth and set with silverware and china plates. Bread, butter and platters full of cold cuts were spread before us. Additional food could be ordered from the polite waiters. At times I took some buttered white bread with me when I left so I could eat it later in the day. But it did not last long. After just a few times, the waiters became suspicious, and forbade my new friend from bringing me to these privileged accommodations. He argued with them and underlined his arguments with a tip. It did not help. I could not return. While it lasted, it had been a nice break for me from the crowded tables and the tasteless food below.

I explored the ship from one end to the other. I met again the children with whom I had traveled on the train to Genoa and also others, some from Königsberg. All of us were going to the same destination, Chile. We played together and became friends, just as my parents made friends with their parents. On deck there were cables and tows everywhere, life boats were hanging on the sides, lounge chairs were set out in long rows where passengers, covered with blankets, rested, read or conversed with each other. There was even a small swimming pool, but I rarely used it. Often I just stood at the ship's railing and looked out over the endless water with nothing in sight, but every once in a while I'd see another ship and sometimes I'd watch the fish that accompanied our own. Sunrise and sunset were my favorite times, especially when the sea was calm. I visited the engine room deep down in the bowels of the ship where sweating sailors fed coal into ovens whose fiery, red hot openings looked to me as if I had descended to the very entrance of hell. It was a never ending adventure without a boring moment.

As we approached the American continent, my interest shifted from the ship to the land. One evening we arrived at the Panama Canal. Passage through the canal was scheduled for the next day. I was up early the following morning, ran out of the cabin, skipped breakfast and spent the next hours on deck watching this wide ship make its way through the narrow canal and its locks. The ship entered the first lock on the Atlantic entrance, its sides inches away from the walls of the lock. The gates closed and the water level in the lock rose slowly and raised this huge and heavy ship as if it were a toy boat in a bathtub. This was repeated three times, and when it was over the ship was eighty-five feet higher than when it had entered the canal. At the other end, about fifty miles away, the same procedure took place in reverse as the ship was now lowered down to the level of the Pacific Ocean. Lush vegetation on both sides of the canal accompanied our passage. I discovered new, strange looking trees I had not seen before. They were palm trees, which from now on became a common sight wherever we went.

On the Pacific side of the canal we disembarked at our first Latin-American town, Balboa. Soon there would be others, little port cities with names such as Guayaquil and Callao. They all had one thing in common. They were ever so different from the European cities and villages we had known up to now. The houses were small and primitive. Most roads were unpaved, had large holes and frequently were littered with refuse and other dirt. Many of the people were poorly dressed. My parents were discouraged, they expected this to foretell what their own future would be like. My reaction was different. I was fascinated by what I saw and gave no thought to a future that was still too far away for me to worry about.

Traders in little boats came alongside the ship as soon as we pulled into a port. They traded local fruit and handicrafts, shouting back and forth to bargain with the passengers high up on the ship for whatever they were willing to give in exchange for the offered wares. In our cabin, my parents discussed what of our belongings they could trade. In Balboa, my father decided to trade his straw hat for a bunch of bananas. I went up on the deck with him and watched as he bent over the railing to bargain with a trader down below. The bargaining was all done with fingers, neither understood the language of the other. After my father was satisfied that he would receive sufficient bananas for his hat, he dropped it into the boat and the trader lifted the fruit up to him on a long pole. It was the first fresh fruit we had eaten since leaving Europe. All along the deck similar transactions were taking place. Other passengers acquired little carvings, embroidery or fruit, just as my father had done. It was a scene that was repeated from now on wherever we entered a port.

After six weeks we arrived in Valparaiso, Chile's main port. It was the end of our long trip. For me it had been a new and exciting experience, an unforgettable adventure. True, like so many others, we were now destitute refugees, unable to communicate with the local population and faced with an uncertain future. But our lives were safe from the war and persecutions raging in Europe. Of our friends and family, we were the last to escape.

To introduce us to our new country, we were met in Valparaiso by a young woman whom we did not know. Her presence had been arranged back home. She accompanied us to a hotel and the next day came with us on the four-hour train ride to Santiago, our final destination. She took us to a *pensión* where we would live and have our meals for the next few months. All these arrangements had been made for us in far off Germany. They now came to an end. We were left to face our future by ourselves. We had arrived. I was eleven-and-a-half years old.

Puro Chile…

A Fresh Start in a New Land

"*P*URO CHILE.*" THUS BEGINS CHILE'S NATIONAL ANTHEM. PURE CHILE: not always pure, not always the "*asilo contra la opresión*" (the asylum against oppression) as a later verse of the anthem claims. But in 1939, at the time of greatest need, Chile did provide the asylum that saved our family and many, many others.

Puro Chile; it was a truly beautiful country we came to. The anthem celebrates Chile's blue skies, fields bordered by flowers, majestic mountains and the sea that bathes it with serenity. In short, the anthem celebrates a blissful imitation of the Garden of Eden. Again and again I confirmed the truth of what the anthem so lovingly expresses.

Yet Chile had not been my parents' first choice, or any kind of choice. It was thrust upon us by the Jewish community in Königsberg in an effort to help us at a time when we needed to leave in a hurry. In mid-1939, eight months after the November Pogrom, German Jews were desperate. It did not matter where— Shanghai or South America—the need was to get away, far away. So my parents gratefully accepted the opportunity to go to Chile. Most countries of the world had closed their doors to refugees, but Chile was an exception, opening its doors for a short time just in time for us.

From the railroad station in Santiago, still accompanied by our guide, we made our way by streetcar to the *Pensión Guttmann*, a boarding house where only other recent immigrants were in residence. We were shown to our room on the second floor, one room for the entire family. The young woman who was our guide said good-bye and left. We were now on our own. I try to imagine what must have gone through my parents' minds at that moment: we faced a future without money, without knowing anything of the country we had come to and we were unable to speak the language. My parents were no longer young. In 1939 my mother was fifty-three and my father fifty-five. Yet soon, in a matter of days, this single room that combined bed and family room was also to become a work room; a mini-factory occupied by a large work table, a machine to cut cloth and two sewing machines. My parents decided that they would earn a living by starting a factory for women's wear that would make dresses, blouses and aprons. This "factory" provided us with our means of survival during our entire stay in Chile. It was an incredibly difficult beginning.

A remarkable communal self-help organization, the *Comité Israelita de Socorro* (*CISROCO*), the Israelite Aid Committee, helped my parents make their decision a reality. It supported many of the new immigrants after their arrival.

CISROCO not only paid for the sustenance that kept the immigrants' bodies and souls together, it also provided loans for the fledgling enterprises the newcomers established to build their economic futures. It was *CISROCO* that provided money for our two sewing machines, the cutting machine, the materials needed for the production and the initial wages for the factory personnel, which consisted of two seamstresses and a cutter.

We settled into the routine of the rooming house. Its daily rhythm was ruled by a gong that sounded for lunch and dinner. I was always hungry so I raced to the dining room as soon as I heard the gong. The dining room quickly filled up with the other thirty or so immigrants who lived in the house. The food we ate was very different from anything I had known before. It was prepared differently, with oil instead of butter, with different spices and new ways of cooking. I ate food that I did not know even existed, particularly vegetables and fruit that did not have a name in the German language.

During and after the meal, the adults exchanged information and shared concerns common to all. The most important topic was how to earn a living. They also commented on the latest news from Europe, the progress of the war and how to help friends and family get out of Germany. Other important topics of conversation included the new German-speaking Jewish congregation, religious services and schools for the children. The table talk was in German, since none of us knew Spanish. I sometimes stayed to listen and realized that the concerns of the other families were not much different from our own. One of the lodgers was the friendly young man who had invited me to lunch in the first-class section of the *Conte Grande*. One day he suddenly fell from his chair in the dining room, and lay on the floor writhing and foaming at the mouth. I was frightened and rushed to his side to see if I could help, but some of the adults were already there. I had never seen an epileptic attack before. I thought he was dying. I was equally frightened during each of his subsequent attacks, but at least I knew that he would recover.

A few days after we arrived, I came down with stomach cramps followed by severe diarrhea. Soon my brother and my parents were similarly sick. We all suffered from what was euphemistically known as *die Chilenische Krankheit* (the Chilean Disease), a recurring and debilitating diarrhea that lasted anywhere from a few days to a few weeks. Most newcomers suffered from it. It was caused by organisms in the water that were different from those in Europe. In time we adapted to them, but for a while, day or night, there were always people waiting in line to use the only toilet on our floor. The bathroom facilities were shared by fifteen or more people. Downstairs, it was the same.

In addition to the diarrhea, there was yet another torture. I woke up during my first night itching all over. When I turned on the light I saw dozens of small, flat, brown insects on my sheets. They were bedbugs. They bred in the cracks of the wooden bed frames, crawling out at night to mercilessly bite the sleeper who would then no longer be able to sleep, but scratched at the bites until the skin was bloody. Bedbugs were common to the older houses in the city, and they survived all the means used to exterminate them, coming back again and again for fresh attacks. In the morning I called the house servant, the *mozo*. He understood my problem, and he used a drastic form of extermination. He pulled the bed frame into the hall in front of our room, doused the joints with kerosene and set it on fire. The fire extinguished itself quickly, burning the kerosene but not the frame and the bedbugs were momentarily vanquished for a few days. They quickly returned, and the process was repeated. I had a vision that if the house was ever burned down, out of the ashes there would emerge a triumphant column of bedbugs ready to invade the adjacent house and join the bedbugs already there.

I had plenty of opportunities to look around in this strange building. Standing in the entrance hall it felt as if I were on a patio, except the patio was indoors. I could see all the rooms at once around the patio, four to a wall, upstairs and down. On the ground floor, in one corner diagonally across, was the dining room. In another corner there was a passage that lead to the kitchen and service quarters. The stairs to the second floor led to a balcony with railings that surrounded the patio. The upstairs rooms opened onto the balcony, while the downstairs rooms opened directly onto the patio. Our room was located over the dining room. One day I was standing idly at the railing, knocking my knee against one of its heavy wooden support beams, when suddenly it came loose and crashed onto the floor below. It barely missed my friend from the ship who was standing underneath.

Our room was a corner room with windows on two sides. Through these windows I had the most spectacular view imaginable of the snow capped Andes mountains, the *Cordillera de los Andes*. In the early summer, the air was clear and free of smog, and as the sun set I would stand at the windows and admire the awesome spectacle of the mountains. They glowed as if made of pure gold.

I saw a different spectacle looking down on the street through these same windows. The house was located at the busiest intersection of Santiago, flanked on one side by the most important business street that had banks, stores and the stock exchange, and on the other side by a wide avenue that traversed the entire city from east to west. Two policemen on elevated stands went crazy trying to control the busses, cars, streetcars and the pedestrians, none of whom paid attention to the policemen. There were no traffic lights anywhere in Santiago. Years later the Jewish community gave a gift to the city. It was the first traffic light ever in Chile, and it was installed at this particular intersection.

When we first arrived, our room was furnished with a bed on each of three walls, two or three chairs and a table in the center. A few days later the table and chairs were pushed aside, and the center of the room was occupied by the factory. It was a busy room during the week without rest or relaxation. The day started early. My fourteen-year-old brother got up to go to work in an automobile repair shop, and as soon as my parents were up they busied themselves with work related to the factory—getting the materials ready that were to be used that day and preparing the samples needed to make sales. I had to get up before the seamstresses and the cutter arrived. As soon as the cutter entered, she started the cutting machine, which was loud enough to be heard in all the neighboring rooms. It was also dangerous. One time she slipped and cut off the tip of a finger. A similar accident happened to my father when he tried to use the machine. The two seamstresses also started their sewing machines. Other seamstresses who were homeworkers arrived in a steady progression to pick up materials for assembly in their own homes. They would return the next day to deliver their finished products and pick up new material. If we were sick, we stayed in bed among all this activity. One time when I had the mumps, I suffered for several days, unable to obtain any relief from the noise made by the machines and the coming and going of all the people.

A few weeks after our arrival someone, perhaps another immigrant, gave me boxes of razor blades to peddle to earn some spending money. I was as yet unable to pronounce the Spanish word for razor blades (*hojas de afeitar*). I walked from store to store in Santiago's commercial center trying to make a sale. The stores were small, and many were owned by Jews and *"Turcos,"* who were actually Arab immigrants from Lebanon, Palestine and Syria, but not from Turkey as the commonly used term suggested. Surprisingly, I was able to sell some of my merchandise, probably because the buyers took pity on a poor immigrant child. At the end of the day, I had earned a little money. I spent it on a pound of liverwurst and took it back to my mother in the *pensión* as a surprise. That evening she prepared the open-faced sandwiches we had always liked so much in Germany but were unknown in Chile. She was touched by my unexpected thoughtfulness. It remained a one time event that was never repeated.

Although we left the pensión for an apartment after a few months, the way my parents conducted their business did not change. My father carried samples in a heavy suitcase from store to store to obtain orders. Most of the stores were small, family-owned businesses. Sometimes he succeeded, in spite of his almost total inability to understand or communicate in the strange language of this strange country. The orders were typically for a dozen aprons or a half-dozen dresses. Just before Independence Day on September 18th, the *Dieciocho,* he received an order for Chilean flags. They were easy to make: three fields, one blue, one white, one red and a single white star on the blue field in the upper left hand corner. The star was the difficult part. Few seamstresses could sew a symmetric star with crisp borders, and the buyers often complained. In the beginning my father delivered the merchandise himself and he received notes payable for up to six months in return. If the buyer's credit rating was good, the banks accepted the notes at a discount in exchange for cash. This discount cut into the meager profits of the business. If the buyer defaulted and did not pay the note, my father was responsible to cover the loss at the bank. This way of operating the business—obtaining orders, delivering the merchandise and then being paid with notes that sometimes defaulted—continued through all ten years of the factory's existence.

During vacations or in the afternoons when I was not in school, I helped my father carry the suitcases, deliver merchandise or pick up the bales of material he bought from wholesalers. I quickly learned the language and often translated for my father when he dealt with customers.

I got to know the city outside the commercial center in yet another way. Sometimes the seamstresses who took their work home with them were late in returning, or did not return at all. It was left to me to find them and retrieve the materials from them, finished or unfinished. The seamstresses were poor and they lived in impoverished residential neighborhoods all over Santiago. My searches took me through neighborhoods and streets that seemed to exist in a different world from the shops, banks and businesses at the center of the city. Some of the residential neighborhoods I visited had streets teeming with unwashed children in ragged clothing. I'd find the women working in dark, windowless rooms lit by a single bulb hanging from the ceiling. Sometimes I retrieved materials that they had not even started to work on. At other times all I could do was to urge them to finish what they had already started. I had never seen such poverty and I was appalled by the horrible squalor.

Other seamstresses lived in more commercial areas, with small stores and repair shops. I'd walk by the shops and look into them with curiosity. The repair shops were invariably tiny, windowless, dark and dirty, and run by one or two mechanics in grimy clothes with faces black from dust and oil. I'd also pass small, dirty restaurants where I did not dare to touch the food. If I bought a soft drink I'd drink it out of the bottle. Small factories polluted the air with their chemical odors and the water with industrial wastes. Adjacent to some commercial areas were red light districts, their lights lit to beckon clients at night. The seamstresses who lived in these neighborhoods were equally poor, and their children just as ragged as those in the residential neighborhoods. They were all part of the one million people that populated Santiago, where the majority of the population was poor.

To reach my destinations I always used streetcars or busses. On many busy corners a bus would come by every minute, and sometimes several busses would arrive at the same time headed for the same destination. Most of the busses were antiquated and their exhaust discharged tons of smoke and particles into the air. There were two types of busses. One was called a *micro* and was small, carrying only seated passengers. The *micro* cost five times as much as the ordinary bus, and it served businessmen and professionals. The regular bus was for the "common people," and it was the one I used. At times the busses were so crowded that riders stood on the running boards holding on to anything they could use to get a grip. I could not get on the crowded busses with my suitcases and packages, and I was frequently left standing on the street for a long wait. Each bus had a driver and a fare collector. The fare collector was a boy who issued tickets and shouted the destination of the bus at every corner. I got to know some of the fare collectors and drivers on the routes I used most often. I'd pay my fare and receive a ticket, and when I got off I'd give the ticket back to the fare collector so that he could sell it again and pocket the money. In return, he would sometimes let me ride for free. We'd share the benefits of this system, but in doing so we had to be careful. If the collector was caught by a *serrucho* (inspector) he would be fined and fired. We had a special hand-and-eye signal and would murmur the warning, "*serrucho,*" if an inspector was present. On those occasions I would pay my fare and keep the ticket when I got off. The same system was used on the overcrowded streetcars. I was never caught, but one day I got off the bus and discovered that my wallet had been stolen. There was no monetary loss because I did not have any money, but it was the first of many wallets I lost to pickpockets. Chilean pickpockets were incredibly skillful, masters at their trade.

I was aware that the existence of our family depended on the factory. Nevertheless, I thought of the business as a demeaning experience: the selling and the bargaining about the sales price of the merchandise, followed by the bargaining about the terms of payment, the pleading and the show of false friendliness to obtain a coveted order before the competition did. To obtain orders in the larger stores, my father gave boxes of candy to the mostly female buyers as a small and friendly bribe, which often smoothed the process.

Over time business improved, but it was never enough to ward off the threat of failure and bankruptcy. This was a constant concern. Some additional people were employed: a representative was hired who sold the products in other cities of the country with varying degrees of success, and a *mozo,* a laborer was hired, who cleaned the premises, carried the sample suitcases, and delivered the merchandise. He also prepared packages to be delivered to other cities and carried them to the railroad station for shipment. Sometimes the *mozo* would disappear along with the merchandise, never to be found again.

My parents worked long hours every day. During our first few years in Chile they would often work seventeen hours a day, seven days a week. The only time they would take off would be for the Jewish High Holidays. The business did not yield enough to enable them to hire more help and provide relief from the terrible workload. By 1942 we had moved from our first apartment into a small house in a somewhat better neighborhood. It was then, almost bankrupt, that they bought a small luncheonette located a few blocks from our house. My mother worked at the luncheonette, and my father at the factory. I helped out at the luncheonette store after school and my father helped at night after his factory business was concluded. I served the few customers who came to eat or drink, made sandwiches to go, sold soft drinks, beer, cookies and chocolate over the counter, and then helped clean up after closing. One Sunday some cadets from the police academy came in to buy ham sandwiches. While slicing the ham, I cut myself. I wrapped my bleeding finger in a handkerchief and finished making the sandwiches in full view of the cadets. Afterwards I wondered if they ever ate the sandwiches. They never came back. Trucks came to deliver cases of soft drinks, boxes of cookies, beer and bread, and the drivers demanded to be paid in cash. Sometimes there was no cash and they would refuse to leave the goods we had ordered. Once sufficient cash became available I would have to go to the warehouses on a tricycle with a big shelf in front to pick up the goods we needed. In spite of all this work, the luncheonette did not even generate enough business to cover its expenses. It was a desperate time and matters quickly came to a crisis. With my mother close to physical collapse, the store was sold at a loss after less than a year.

My father, now sixty years old, suffered from heart disease. His health was a constant concern. His doctors advised him to stop working so hard, but that was impossible. The factory was the sole source of the family income, and my father was the driving force behind the factory. We could not live without his work. In an attempt to allay their anxiety, my parents took on a new partner. His presence relieved some of the financial worries derived from my father's uncertain state of health. However, sharing the factory income with a partner diminished our already small income. Eventually, this partnership fulfilled its purpose and insured the ongoing existence of the factory.

Refugees in a New Land

How was it that we were able to enter Chile at a time when most other countries had closed their doors to Jewish refugees? In fact, Chile's doors were only open for a short time, and after little more than a year the flow of refugees was once again restricted.[1] I want to tell about how it happened that the doors opened all of a sudden and then, after allowing a few thousand refugees to enter, were just as suddenly closed.

It is impossible to determine how many European Jews found refuge in Chile. Neither the government nor the Jewish community ever produced a complete accounting. It was an impossible task because refugees arrived both legally and illegally. In addition to the legal immigrants, there were those who entered the country on tourist or other restricted visas, and never left. Illegal immigrants also crossed the border from neighboring countries such as Bolivia and Argentina. In addition, some immigrants in transit to Bolivia disembarked in the north of Chile and did not continue on their journey. Estimates of the total Jewish immigration vary widely. One account estimates that 13,000 Jewish immigrants from Central Europe reached Chile between 1933 and 1945. Another source provides a number of 12,000 for 1939 alone. Wojak[2] states that the best estimate is 12,000 Jews from 1938 through 1941. Whatever the number, most of the Jewish refugees were from Germany, which by this time included Austria and Czechoslovakia.

There is a record of the first Jew in Chile,[3] *Don* Francisco Maldonado de Silva, who was born in 1592, incarcerated in Lima, Peru, by the Spanish Inqui-

---

[1] General information on the Jewish exile in Chile and the conditions in the country is based on Irmtrud Wojak, "Exil in Chile—Die deutsch-jüdische und politische Emigration während des Nationalsozialismus 1933–1945," Berlin Metropol Verlag, 1994.

[2] Ibid.

[3] Günther Böhm, Historia de los Judíos en Chile, Volumen 1, Período Colonial, Editorial Andrés Bello, 1984.

sition and in 1639 burned to death at the stake in the same city. More recently, during the early part of the 20th century, there were Jewish immigrations from Russia, Romania, Poland, Turkey and Yugoslavia. Beginning in 1933 immigrants from Germany, refugees from the Nazis, predominated.

During the presidency of Arturo Alessandri from 1932 until 1938, Jewish immigration into Chile was not welcome. For example, in 1933 the foreign minister conveyed a message to the Chilean consul in Berlin instructing him to limit visas provided to "Israelites." Of eighteen visas, he complained, fourteen had been granted to *individuos de esta raza* (individuals of this race). A couple of years later there was an unwritten agreement between the Jewish community and the government to a limit of fifty families per year selected by a special committee of the community. However, this unofficial quota was exceeded during the last years of Allessandri's government when visas were given to approximately 300 families per month, or about 400 to 500 persons.

There were many reasons for this opposition to Jewish immigration. One was the fear of the effect the newcomers would have on the Chilean economy, which had been in crisis since 1932. There was also the anti-Semitism of large segments of the population. Last but not least was the anti-Jewish agitation of the *Movimiento Nacional Socialista* (M.N.S.), the Chilean version of the Nazis founded in 1932 by descendants of earlier German immigrants.

Beginning in the middle of the 19th century, there was a large migration of Germans to Chile. Many of them settled in the south of the country, where the climate was similar to that in Germany. Their descendants maintained a strong German identity, spoke German and identified themselves as *Deutsch-Chilenen* (German-Chileans) rather than as Chileans. In the mid-thirties, they numbered about 30,000. Many of their children went to one of the thirty-six German schools established in Chile where they were taught in German. Some of their teachers had been hired in Germany and were members of the *N.S.D.A.P.*, the *Nationalsozialistische Deutsche Arbeiter Partei,* the German Nazi party. The German-Chileans read special German language newspapers published in Chile, which were generally pro-Nazi and carried Nazi propaganda. Many of them sympathized with the Nazis in Germany. The M.N.S., in turn, supported anti-Jewish campaigns in the press, which were frequently instigated by conservative Catholic and anti-Zionist Arabic circles. Occasionally the M.N.S. found itself involved in political dilemmas. For example, a Nazi youth organization of German-Chileans prohibited its members to marry Chilean women who were not of German origin in order to preserve the purity of the Aryan race. But because the

M.N.S. labeled itself a Chilean party, for obvious political reasons it refused to support that prohibition. Later, after the beginning of the war in Europe, many young German-Chilean men traveled to Germany to fight for their "fatherland", i.e., Germany. I met one of them. He was a friendly young man, a little older than me. Initially I was reluctant to talk to him, as I expected him to be a devout Nazi. His ancestors had come to Chile about eighty years earlier. I was surprised when he explained that he was not a Nazi, and that he did not believe in Nazism, but nevertheless felt himself to be a German rather than a Chilean, and it was that loyalty that motivated him. He felt that his fatherland needed him. After the war I saw him again. He had come back disappointed because he had not been accepted as a full German due to his Chilean birth. Perhaps the outcome of the war also had an effect on him. At any rate, he now felt that he was more of a Chilean than had been the case when he left to fight the war.

In November 1938, a new government came to power in Chile. The new president, Pedro Aguirre Cerda, was elected at the head of a center-left coalition, the *Frente Popular* (the Popular Front). Aguirre Cerda was sympathetic to the plight of the Jews in Germany. Under his leadership the window was opened that allowed thousands of new Jewish immigrants into the country. But soon there was a backlash. The leader of the M.N.S., Jorge González von Marées, who had been elected to Congress, sued the foreign minister over the massive influx of immigrants. The foreign minister was forced to resign in February of 1940. As a result, the window closed, and except for the 1,637 more Jews who managed to find refuge in Chile during the next two years, no additional Jewish immigrants were admitted. The window, open during fourteen crucial months, enabled thousands of Jews to escape certain death. I was among them together with my family.

The New Jewish Community

In addition to making a living, new Jewish immigrants wanted to form a community that could satisfy their religious and social needs. That is, they wanted to build a Jewish congregation.[4] Although such congregations had existed in Santiago since the beginning of the century, they did not meet the needs of the new immigrants. For one thing, there was the language problem: the existing Ashkenazi congregations were made up of Jews whose origins were in Eastern Europe and spoke Yiddish. Another congregation was Sephardic and was made up of Jews who were descendants of those expelled from Spain in 1492. Instead of Yid-

---

[4] Wojak, op. cit.

dish, their language was Ladino, which was closely related to Spanish. My parents, like most of the newcomers, spoke neither. Their language was German. In addition to the difference in languages, the religious rites of these two communities were also different from each other, and different from the rites we had brought with us from Germany. Finally, our economic and cultural integration into the customs of this new land presented problems that were beyond the understanding of the older, well-established Jewish communities.

German refugees who arrived before the mass immigration of the late thirties had founded a federation of German-speaking Jews in 1935. It came to a premature end in early 1938 due to a lack of interest. Later the same year a small group of immigrants founded a new organization for religious, cultural and funeral purposes, the Congregation *B'ne Jisroel*. Only 150 persons took part in the first general meeting of this fledgling organization. In 1940, at the time my parents joined, there were almost 400 heads of family or single adults who had become members. At the end of 1944, membership had grown to 1,539. There were similar, smaller congregations in other Chilean cities with German-Jewish immigrants.

My parents attended religious services in the synagogue of this congregation. I rarely accompanied them, but when I did it seemed as if I was back in Königsberg. I listened to the same prayers and heard the same melodies. It was a "liberal" congregation, but even so, my mother had to sit in a different place from my father and me. Two young rabbis, both recent immigrants, performed the services in German with the exception of the Hebrew prayers. It was in this synagogue that I had my *Bar Mitzvah* on May 24, 1941. Every Sabbath a different portion from the first five books of the Hebrew Bible, the *Torah,* and a selection from the prophetic books of the Bible, the *Haftorah*, were chanted in the synagogue. As is customary for a *Bar Mitzvah* boy, on this morning I chanted both of them, in addition to chanting the required blessings. I must have done well because right after the *Bar Mitzvah* the rabbis asked me to become a *chasan* (cantor) at the special youth services held on Saturday afternoons. I accepted and in the process even became moderately religious. It did not last long. My own inclinations and the influence of the atheistic Zionist youth movement that I had joined were stronger than my religious feelings, and I soon gave up my cantorial responsibilities.

Though I did not often go with my parents to religious services, I did join them for the many cultural events organized by the congregation. There were lectures, theater performances, concerts and sometimes performances of complete

Viennese operettas that were accompanied by a piano rather than an orchestra. The performers and the lecturers were former university professors, actors and singers, supported by talented amateurs, all of whom were members of the congregation. I had met them all at one time or another. All of these performances and lectures were in German, as most of the audience did not understand any other language. I was greatly interested in all these functions, and I enjoyed them very much. Previously I had been too young to participate in such activities, but now that I was getting older I was eager to absorb the culture that was my natural heritage along with the Judaic culture into which I had been born.

Membership in the congregation was not free. For many years my parents could not afford the fee. Their business barely earned enough for food and other essentials—and sometimes not even that. Many times my father had to meet with a synagogue official to request a reduction or elimination of the fee. It must have been difficult for my proud father to have to demean himself year after year. During most of the year, religious services were poorly attended. It was different for the High Holidays, *Rosh Hashanah*, the Jewish New Year, and *Yom Kippur*, the Day of Atonement, that followed ten days later. On these two holidays, everybody wanted to attend. The synagogue facilities were much too small to accommodate everyone. Extra services were held in rented facilities, such as movie theaters, and tickets were sold. My parents did not have the money to buy tickets, so my father had to repeat the pilgrimage and ask for free or reduced price tickets. A few years earlier my parents had been active philanthropists, but now they were at the other end of the stick and became recipients of the generosity of others.

In some years I volunteered to sing in the high holiday choir. I loved to sing the traditional melodies. The father of my closest friend was a trained opera singer, although in exile he manufactured chocolate bars. He led one of the overflow services. I loved to hear him sing and it was in his choir that I participated with great enthusiasm. In those years when I did not participate, my parents still expected me to attend services. Many of my friends were similarly forced to go to the synagogue. None of us were believers. We went to the services, but spent most of our time talking outside. *Yom Kippur* is a fast day. Observant Jews do not eat for twenty-four hours. They attend the evening services when the holiday begins and then spend the whole next day in the synagogue. But we were teenage rebels, opposed to religion. On that day we left the synagogue during the lunch hour to buy rich sandwiches. Our rebellion was limited though. We ate the sandwiches in a nearby park and not in front of the synagogue. By doing this I felt that I was asserting my independence, rejecting what I felt were obsolete beliefs and superstitions that did not apply to me. Yet I also felt guilty for breaking the injunction not to eat on *Yom Kippur*, which I had been brought up with and accepted until that time. In the end, though, rebellion won out. I never again fasted on *Yom Kippur*.

Kidma: A Zionist Alternative

The congregation with its synagogue was for grownups. I wanted to be with other children my age who were Jewish and spoke German. I attended Hebrew school at the synagogue, but that was just another school. There was an alternative. I joined a Zionist youth group called *Kidma,* a name derived from the Hebrew word *kadima* (forward). The group was founded in 1939 by a few immigrant teenagers and young adults. The goal was to bring about the creation of a Jewish state in Palestine and encourage members to move there—to "make *aliyah,*" a traditional expression that means "go up (to Jerusalem)." Joining the *Kidma* was a fateful decision that came to dominate my life in Chile and beyond.

We quickly grew to about 100 members, ranging in age from pre- to late-teens, and all of us were from German immigrant families. Our parents were not concerned about whether their children would be asked to make *aliyah* in the future. They were more interested in providing us with a positive Jewish environment, keeping us off the streets and preventing us from mingling with the unknown, and seemingly unknowable, Chilean environment. There were no other Jewish youth groups at this time. Later, other youth groups appeared that did not demand a Zionist commitment. Instead, they provided a pleasant social environment for their members. Many of the children and teenagers who initially joined the *Kidma* left our organization and became members of these other groups. I stayed.

Initially, the *Kidma* was purely an immigrant organization and we only spoke German. But after a few years, young people from the older Jewish community joined the *Kidma* and in time more and more Spanish was spoken. This transition was not an easy one. We were used to our own circle of friends and our own ways. The newcomers brought not only their language with them, but their own different background and culture. Some of us resisted and coined an ironic name for them. We called them *plumeros* (feather dusters), derived from Indian feather headdresses. The name stuck and became commonly used by the Chileans and Germans alike.

In the beginning, I joined a group of twelve other boys—all of us eleven or twelve years old. There was a similar group of girls. Later these groups combined and became coeducational. Each group was called a *kvutzah* (a community), and each had a special name. Once we were combined with the girls, my group was known as "The Chain," or *Shalshelet* in Hebrew, which was symbolic of links that would never break. Other groups formed with names such as "The Flame" or "The Future." These groups were separated by age, with three years of difference between each level. Each group had a leader who was a member of one age level above its own. Some of these groups used Spanish as their language, but others, including mine, spoke German to the end. We never admitted a *plumero*. In the beginning, the oldest members, the leaders of the whole organization, were between seventeen and nineteen years old.

We met once or twice a week, first in the rooms of one of the other Jewish organizations, but later in a house specially rented by the *Kidma*. We sang, played games and danced the *horrah* (the Jewish national folk dance). There were flags and uniforms—all the trappings the scouts used in their organization. But to us they also had a deeper meaning. I was proud when I wore the uniform of blue pants and a white shirt with a blue kerchief around my neck. Blue and white were the colors of Zionism; blue and white were the colors of the Zionist flag.

Right from the beginning we were taught a few words of Hebrew and a little grammar. Our group leader told us about a Viennese Jew by the name of Theodor Herzl who, at the turn of the century, had developed the idea of founding a Jewish state in Palestine. He wrote a couple of books that became the first Zionist texts. Then there was the story about a one-armed hero in Palestine who led a fight against Arabs in the 1920s. Unfortunately, he died in the process. His name was Trumpeldor. We frequently sang a song about him. Other stories were told about a new, ideal way of living in a collective community called a *kibbutz*. To me this was all fresh and exciting, and at the age of twelve I longed to become part of this world. All these stories and the insistence that we, young Jews, were the future pioneers who would build a new and perfect society in a Jewish homeland gave me a new pride in being Jewish. That was important. The sense of being in the forefront of safeguarding the future of the Jews was a powerful antidote for the feelings of inferiority I had developed in Germany due to the Nazi propaganda, and helped me to regain my self-esteem.

Not entirely, however. For many years when I met outsiders, Chileans, I continued to deny—even under the most implausible circumstances—that I was Jewish. Neighbors, salesgirls in stores and students in the schools I attended would ask me about it, and I would say no, I was not Jewish. It must have been obvious that I was lying, but I could not help myself. For a long time I continued to feel inferior, ashamed of being recognized as a Jew. The Nazi propaganda had left wounds that cut me deeply.

There were many weekends when we hiked to the mountains surrounding Santiago. Sometimes a few of us went, sometimes larger groups. At times I went by myself; I didn't want company. We went up the mountains, into the valleys between them, to hot mineral springs that bubbled out of the ground, to lakes and meadows and to abandoned mines. We went for one day, or two, or three or even more. For one day hikes I carried a sandwich, some fruit, a bottle of water. For longer hikes we carried all we needed on our backs: pots for cooking, food supplies, water, blankets and tents. Our equipment was heavy and primitive. It was cheap; few of us had any money. Much of it was army surplus. Instead of sleeping bags, we used blankets. The canvass tents were heavy and so were the wooden stakes. Cooking utensils were ordinary kitchenware. Hiking boots were important. At one time I had a pair made to measure, even though I could hardly afford them. When the boots were finished however, they were less comfortable than the store bought pair I had been using. I only wore them once or twice and then discarded them. Sometimes we had to take special measures to compensate for what we lacked. One time I joined three other boys to climb a peak near Santiago called *San Ramón*, which was about 10,000 feet high. It was to be a two-day hike. We knew it would be cold so we armed ourselves with some bottles of *pisco*, a strong liquor that is a Chilean national drink even though it originates in Peru. The *pisco* was to keep us warm at night when neither tent nor blankets would. Unfortunately, it did not. We shivered through the night and hardly slept. But the next day we reached the peak and returned home with a feeling of great accomplishment.

One Sunday I woke up early. I was upset about something that had happened the previous day, but I don't recall what it was. I wanted to be alone that day and decided to go on a hike. I got dressed, prepared some food, filled my water bottle and set out without telling anybody where I was going. I took a streetcar to the end of the line at the foot of the mountains and started to hike. I walked through a forest of small trees, passed by a tiny and dirty pond and then started a steep climb up a narrow ravine lined with small bushes. After a while I came to a big rock that we called the "House of Rocks," the *Casa de Piedras*. Just beyond this point I reached the tree line, where the vegetation ended and the ravine opened onto a steep field of stones that ended in a ridge. It opened up like a fan, and we knew this field and this ridge as the "Fan," the *Abanico*. It was a short climb to the top. All this was familiar territory. I had been here many times before. About three hours had passed since I started the hike. Once I reached the top of the ridge I decided to try something new. Instead of going back down the way I had come, I decided to descend down the other side of the ridge. None of us had ever explored this territory, and I had no idea where it would lead me or what I would find along the way. Briefly the thought crossed my mind that this was dangerous. Nobody knew where I was, and if I got hurt there was no one who could help me in these lonely mountains. On the way up, I had not met another person. But at sixteen it was easy to dismiss such thoughts. I decided to proceed. I climbed down another field of stones, steeper and longer than the one I had climbed up. At the bottom I found myself on a footpath into a valley that sloped gently downhill. A bubbling brook accompanied the path on the right. I was surrounded by blooming cacti and flowery vegetation—a sea of purple, red, yellow and white. I followed this delightful path for a couple of hours, stopping frequently to take in the peace that nature offered: the murmurs from the brook, the riot of color, the high cliffs on both sides. I was sorry when the path ended in the unfamiliar outskirts of Santiago. The adventure was over. It had been a great day and with it my spirits had been restored.

Often on our hikes we met peasants who offered us samples of the vegetables and goat cheese they produced. One time, when our own food had run out, a peasant woman in a shack we passed on the path cooked a *cazuela de ave* for us, a rich Chilean soup made from vegetables, rice and chicken. We ate it while listening to Mendelsohn's violin concerto on her radio in a hut on a desolate mountain path! I can still picture the strange scene. There we were, eight boys and girls, fifteen or sixteen years old, dirty, tired, hungry and thirsty after a long hike, sitting in a shack open to the weather on wooden boxes around a wooden plank supported by similar boxes. One of us idly twiddled the dial of the radio in the corner. All of a sudden there emerged those melodies that we knew and loved. The woman outside preparing the meal at an open fire was probably illiterate and used to nothing but Chilean dances and songs, *cuecas* and *tonadas,* and she was probably hearing classical music for the first time ever. What a contrast! I could not tear myself away from the music, but at the same time I kept thinking about the unbridgeable gap that separated us from her and her life. We finished our *cazuela* just as the concerto ended, paid the friendly woman and went on, satisfied and exhilarated by the experience.

Another time four of us hitchhiked to the coast and then hiked for several days along the beaches. We went swimming and boating, and lay on the sand long enough to acquire painful sunburns. We cooked our meals on the beaches. The food was so bad that it upset my stomach for months after the hike was over.

Late one night, in a village near the city of Valparaiso, we needed a place to sleep. At the jail we asked if they had an empty cell. They did not. All of the cells were occupied by drunks. The jailer suggested that we try the army barracks. We had more luck there and spent the night on a straw covered floor.

Years later Santiago expanded and our hiking destinations were transformed into urban areas. The old hiking paths became streets, while bushes, wild flowers, goat shelters and vegetable plots were replaced by expensive houses and elegant shopping malls. Hikers to areas that had escaped urbanization were more likely to encounter robbers instead of the friendly goat shepherds who had offered us cheese. Some hikers returned without their clothes because the robbers had taken them along with their money. I was sad when I heard about this during one of my later visits to Chile. By this time, the population had grown from one million to over five million. The city had also grown to accommodate the new inhabitants, and in the process had swallowed many of the areas that in former times had offered us unique and treasured adventures.

One of our older leaders had the idea to form a youth orchestra. The twelve or so players were all about my age, fourteen and fifteen years old. The quality of the orchestra can be gauged by the fact that I played the violin in it. I had not progressed since my two years of lessons back in 1937 and 1938, and I had not taken any additional lessons since then. I hadn't even practiced on my own. But the other "musicians" were no better. Generally, we played simple songs: Zionist and German folk music and old Jewish melodies. We also played one piece that was a bit more ambitious, the "Toy Symphony," which was once thought to have been composed by Haydn, but was actually written by Leopold Mozart, the father of Wolfgang Amadeus Mozart. It was a relatively simple symphony that featured water pipes used to produce bird calls and other special effects by nonmusical devices. Although we must have sounded awful, we were invited to play on the radio in the *Hora Hebrea*, the weekly "Jewish Hour" that was broadcast on one of the Santiago stations. One Sunday morning we all went to the studio, tuned our instruments and then the announcer told the audience about the children's orchestra that was made up of refugee kids. We were nervous because practically the whole Jewish community of Santiago listened to the *Hora Hebrea*. I don't know how well we performed, but the next day there was a picture in one of the newspapers showing us playing in the studio. We had not even noticed the presence of a photographer.

Beginning in 1942, the *Kidma* organized annual summer camps that provided us with vacations that otherwise would have been out of reach for many of us. Because of the *Kidma* participants who lacked the resources to pay for the camp, we were able to tap into the resources of the Jewish community and found ways to collect enough to cover the costs. I missed the first summer camp because I was in bed with yellow jaundice. But I participated the next year, and in most of the following years. For the first few summers the camp was located on an open field that had been leased from the landowner. The site was located in a river valley near Santiago called *Cajón del Maipo.* In 1943 I volunteered to help set up the camp, and I left the city a few days prior to opening day. It took a little over two hours to get there, traveling by bus and a narrow gauge railway. I got off the train in a little village about a mile from the camp site and then walked along the river—with high mountains rising just beyond the opposite bank—to join the others already at the camp. The building materials had been brought in earlier by truck and included tents, wood, tools and supplies. We put up the big tents in which up to twenty people could sleep, with boys and girls of the same group together in one tent. We prepared the cooking facilities, benches, tables and whatever else was needed for the camp to operate. Of great importance was the flagpole we erected. The flag was an essential component of the camp. After a few days, the camp was ready to receive its occupants.

The camp was rather primitive, but nevertheless provided us with a unique experience in outdoor living and companionship, complete with camp fires, group singing, sports and hikes into surrounding areas. Like everybody else, I performed chores on a rotating basis. There was no outside help to do the work. I served at the table, helped in the kitchen, washed the dishes, cleaned the camp and performed a two-hour shift of watch duty at night during which I would walk around the camp with a flashlight. We had no weapons and if a serious problem ever arose, all we could have done would have been to shout for help. But nothing ever happened. There was one older couple who were members of the Movement and already had children themselves. The wife was in charge of the kitchen. Every day she prepared food for the fifty or sixty (or some summers up to 100) of us who came to the tables ravenously hungry after the day's activities. She ordered most of the food from the nearby village. In the morning, we listened for the train whistle and then ran to unload the supplies when the train made a special stop at the camp site to deliver food and mail.

Each morning we attended a ceremony at which the Zionist flag with its Star of David was raised, and at sundown we were there for the lowering of the flag. We stood in a rectangle around the flagpole, saluted the flag and sang Hebrew songs. Each day one of us was chosen to raise or lower the flag; an honor we all coveted.

When I was sixteen or seventeen, I was appointed treasurer and collected the funds that we used to pay the bills. That year the camp was on a different site, much further away from the city. One week I needed to take a large amount of cash from Santiago to the camp to pay local vendors near the camp site, primarily for food and supplies. The camp was a long way from the nearest railroad station and I had to walk more than three hours in the dark. I was afraid of being robbed and I carried a pistol. I had never used a gun and would not have known what to do with it if I had been assaulted. Crossing a bridge, I did shoot one bullet into the water below just to try out the gun. That gave me some assurance. I was relieved when finally, around midnight, I entered the camp.

One year, a few of us hiked to the border between Argentina and Chile where at a height of 12,000 feet a huge statue of Christ had been erected. On the way we passed through an area where some hotels were being built, and we spent the night in one of the unfinished rooms. The place was called "Portillos" and little did we know that in a few years it would become a world famous ski resort. We were there at its birth. The next morning we left early and carried our backpacks, pots and blankets all the way up the mountain. We barely made it, and when we finally reached the monument we were exhausted. At that height there is little oxygen and breathing is difficult without prior acclimatization. But we were rewarded for our troubles with a spectacular view. We were surrounded by a chain of snow covered mountains, among them the Aconcagua, which includes the highest peak in the Western hemisphere at 23,000 feet. We were stunned by the beauty of the spectacle. After a while we started our descent and once again passed through Portillos. This time we did not stop. Our progress was slow and we realized that the camp was beyond reach for that night. We had not brought tents and looked for an accommodation. Some empty railroad freight cars on a siding provided shelter, and we were fortunate that the cars were not moved during the night.

In August 1943, I was suddenly confronted with a whole new set of goals. The *Kidma* had become affiliated with a worldwide Zionist leftist youth movement, the *Hashomer Hatzaïr* (the Young Guardian), while retaining its original name, *Kidma*. I do not remember how this affiliation came about, whether the older members voted on it, whether they were even consulted, or whether the leadership simply decided it on its own. The *Hashomer Hatzaïr* was the international youth arm of a strong political party in Palestine, *MAPAM*, the United Workers Party, which was oriented towards the Soviet Union. Its goal was a classless society under *kibbutz* leadership. The *Kidma* now became "The Movement." The somewhat unfocused Zionist group I had joined almost four years earlier had been transformed into a dogmatic, left-oriented organization. It adopted the goals of the parent *MAPAM* party: the creation of a socialist society in Palestine, the creation of a "bi-national" state (an unexplained political slogan that I was never able to understand), which was to be governed jointly with the Arabs, and close collaboration with the Soviet Union and Stalin. On this last point, though, there was disagreement among the members. Every year on the anniversary of the Movement, the older members discussed whether we should be for or against Stalin. The discussion always lasted into the wee hours of the morning, but never resolved anything. Every year I attended this discussion and every year I slept through most of it. My mind was made up. Any totalitarian society, right or left, was anathema to me. Stalin's Soviet Union was among the worst. I never understood how any of my companions could think otherwise after having been lucky enough to escape the all too similar Nazi terrorism.

In an effort to raise our consciousness about the theories underlying the Movement's ideology, we began to study the works of Zionist and Socialist thinkers. The themes of our first years in the *Kidma* recurred again and again, always at a higher level, always adding more ideas to our store of knowledge. We ourselves prepared the lectures on these topics and each of us presented his or her assigned subject to our group. I once prepared a lecture about an early theoretician called Chaim Arlosoroff, who wrote his books in the 1920's. I did not understand his ideas, and when I gave my presentation, nobody else did either. Of course all this was not meant to be just theory. The aim was always to get us to Israel and a *kibbutz*.

We were expected not only to join a *kibbutz*, but specifically one affiliated with *MAPAM*. Other more liberal, less militant *kibbutzim* were not acceptable. Rules formulated in a country 6,000 miles away were intruding on our daily lives. These rules prohibited girls from wearing makeup and boys were not permitted to wear ties. Such things were condemned for being "bourgeois." I never learned any ballroom dances because they were equally bourgeois and hence also forbidden. I did dance the *horrah* a lot, which, mercifully, was still allowed. Sexual promiscuity was frowned upon, although sexual relations for unmarried couples who loved each other were "allowed." We did not think about and never mentioned homosexuality.

Of much larger consequence was that higher education was discouraged because the future socialist Palestine needed proletarian laborers and not academicians. At fifteen I was very susceptible to the influence of the Movement—

too susceptible. Accordingly, I terminated my formal education after completing the ninth grade. Not all members were so susceptible. Others continued their education. Those who stayed in school were sometimes tolerated, at other times expelled. There was no consistent policy. In particular, many of the leaders were students who were planning on academic careers. Among them were future doctors, engineers and a seismologist. While those who were "ordinary" members were often expelled, those in the leadership positions were not. In the end, few college educated members, whether leaders or not, actually went on to join a *kibbutz*. The movement's ideology proved a self-fulfilling prophecy: most of those who joined lacked formal higher education. The *kibbutz* at that time did not require such education. Most of its work would be manual or farm labor.

In spite of this I still remained a true, active and faithful member of the Movement. My wake up call had not yet sounded. I supported the expulsion of some of my best friends from the unbreakable "Chain," including two girls who had committed the unpardonable sin of using makeup, and one boy who later became a world renowned psychiatrist, because he insisted on the pursuit of his university studies. Amazingly, these three remained my friends in spite of what I had done to them. Perhaps they were happy to have escaped the pressure and coercion of the ever-more militant Movement.

In September 1944, I was asked to lead one of the younger groups. I was sixteen years old, and those I was assigned to lead were thirteen. The group was particularly difficult and included both boys and girls. Several previous leaders had already failed. The children of this group had two problems: they were undisciplined and unmotivated. The task was beyond my expertise and power. I never succeeded in getting more than five children to attend meetings, although in theory the group included many more than that. Sometimes only two kids would show up. It was a complete failure. I gave up the leadership after four frustrating months and never again tried to lead any groups.

That same year, three of my closest friends and I formed a common cash fund to which each of us contributed all our earnings and withdrew whatever we needed to cover our needs. Later we admitted two girls, one of whom was my girlfriend, Ursel. It was intended to simulate the future when we all would live the collective life of the *kibbutz* and share everything we owned. In fact, it was an artificial game. All along I felt uncomfortable with it and, although we never talked about it, I am sure the others did too. This game lasted for a few months and then fizzled out.

In 1947, I was the first of my generation to be elected to the leadership council of the Movement in Chile, which included a branch in Valparaiso. This was not only an honor, it was a sign of the confidence the members and the leadership placed in me. But I disappointed them all. I had begun to have doubts about what I had so fervently believed up to that time. I wanted to break out of the Movement's limitations and experience life as others on the outside did. I wanted to set my own goals and strive to reach them. I wanted to experiment with lifestyles other than the strict communal life visualized by the organization. It was not yet entirely clear to me exactly what I was looking for, but it was clear that I wanted something other than what I had experienced to date. As a result, I could no longer summon the enthusiasm and commitment needed to be an effective Movement leader. I lasted six months and then resigned from the council.

After World War II was over, the Movement in Chile established a preparatory farm, the *hachsharah*, to prepare its older members for the transition from private life in a Diaspora city to communal living on a *kibbutz* in Palestine. This was mandatory. They were expected to learn both the farming and the collective style of life they would find on a *kibbutz*. Many members followed their ideals and went to *hachsharah*, made *aliyah* and joined a *kibbutz*. Others left the Movement even before the *hachsharah* because they disagreed with the ideology, disliked the idea of the collective life or wanted to pursue professional studies. In 1945, it was the oldest generation comprised of those in their early twenties that went to the farm. My turn came three years later.

Teenager in a Strange Country
The ten years I spent in Chile were especially important because they were the years of my adolescence when I grew from boyhood to adulthood.

It wasn't long before I felt at home in Santiago. I came to know the city and the surrounding villages quickly by helping out in my father's business. I learned first-hand of the unimaginable living conditions that prevailed among the Chilean working class, and I saw their poverty, their unsanitary dwellings, their lack of even the most minimal amenities and their pitifully confined living spaces. I visited seamstresses who were living in hovels that consisted of one- or two-room units surrounding a common patio-like open area. But they had no running water except what was provided by a single tap on the patio. They used common toilets that were shared by all who lived there. Most of the time they cooked their meals outdoors in front of their rooms. Some of the seamstresses I came to know told me that they had given birth to many children—twelve, fifteen, even eighteen—because they lacked knowledge of birth control, which, in any case, was forbidden by the Catholic Church. Most of their children had died from hunger, malnutrition and disease. Few of the women had more than three or four surviving children. There was no divorce in Chile, but men frequently abandoned their wives and went to live with other women who bore them additional children. Many men spent whatever little they earned on drink. Sometimes the women who worked for us came in with a black eye and bruises. Their men came home drunk and beat them. Frequently, it was the women who earned the family keep. Prior to our arrival in Santiago, I never imagined that such living conditions could exist.

There was another class of poor—the lowest of the low. I saw them when I crossed the bridges of the Mapocho River, which divided the city in two. They lived under the bridges. Considered a national symbol, they were "affectionately" called the *roto chileno*, *roto* being the word for broken. They were in rags; they were hungry; they were drunk on cheap wine. When it was cold, they would build a fire under the bridges to keep warm. The *roto chileno* earned a little money walking the streets collecting bottles, rags, old clothes and newspapers, and then reselling them. In the winter when it was cold, some of them would be found dead from exposure.

I observed such conditions day in and day out, and that raised my social consciousness more than any of the Movement's socialist theories. In fact, the Movement did not concern itself with Chilean poverty or local social conditions because its interest was centered on the future Jewish state in Palestine. I cannot remember a single occasion when the Movement got involved in the struggle of Chilean workers in their battles against factory, mining and business owners, who kept them in dire poverty through gross exploitation.

Even though we were poor, we lived a secure life. The war was being fought on distant shores and continents, and although everybody was concerned about friends and family left behind in Europe, we were never in any danger. There were some scarcities, but not many. I frequently did the family shopping and, strangely enough, it was often difficult to find butter. When it was available, the butter was often rancid. There was also a shortage of gasoline, and many cars were converted to run on an alternate fuel that required the installation of an unsightly, external tank mounted on the back of the car. We did not have a car, so this was of no importance to us.

Earthquakes were a constant threat. I experienced my first earthquake shortly after we moved into our first apartment. It was night and I woke to a rumbling noise and saw everything shaking and moving in the room. I did not immediately understand what was happening, but when I finally realized it was an earthquake, I raced into the street in a panic. By that time the shaking had stopped, and all the neighbors were assembled in front of their houses in nightclothes or anything else they were able to grab on their way out. There were many more earthquakes during my stay in Santiago. I felt one in school, standing on a second floor balcony, and in my panic I stayed frozen to the railing unable to move. I felt another sitting on a rock in a brook at one of our summer camps. I never overcame my fear, and I never got used to them. Although the city had not suffered major damage from earthquakes in the past few decades, I could never be sure. One always felt the beginning of an earthquake, but never knew what the ultimate outcome would be. Regions south and north of Santiago had been heavily damaged in recent years. Valparaiso was destroyed in 1907. Another quake on January 24, 1939, killed more than 20,000 people in the southern city of Chillán. For me earthquakes were always a frightening experience. My mother had been right when years earlier she had feared Chile as "the earthquake country."

Our first apartment after the *pensión* was on the ground floor of an older three-story house in a lower middle class area. Its single bedroom, which was located off to the side was reserved for the factory, which still relied on the two sewing machines and cutting table we had used in the *pensión*. We had no telephone, but somehow business functioned without it. Otherwise the apartment was like a railroad flat. From the entrance hall I walked right into the living room, which was used as my parent's bedroom. There was no door in between these two rooms and we used a curtain to provide a nominal bit of privacy. At any time, day or night, I had to pass through this room to get to my bedroom in the maid's quarter in the back, which was reached by a door at the rear of the living/bedroom. My brother and I slept in what had once been the maid's room. We used the primitive maid's bathroom although in front, next to the factory room, there was a bathroom with a tub and shower. Also in the back was the tiny, dark kitchen where my mother prepared our meals. Fortunately, we had a small patio where I could read and study. As in the *pensión,* I was plagued by bedbugs, and there were countless mice. One night I was awakened by something brushing against my leg but did not realize what it was. Days later, when changing the linen, I found an asphyxiated mouse beneath the sheets.

It was here, in this apartment, that I experienced what it meant to be poor. Compared to the poverty of Chilean laborers we were well off, but compared to what I had known previously, this was genuine poverty. Even in the *pensión* we had three meals a day. But at the apartment this was no longer true. When my mother bought grapes, she measured out so many grapes for each of us. Many times, when money was short, small portions of food would be measured out. We had to make do with the clothing we owned, and were only rarely able to buy something new. This was especially important for me because I was still growing and quickly outgrew what I had. My mother worked all day in the factory so we had a maid who came in to do the cleaning. One day she stole 1,000 *pesos* out of a closet. It was not much money because a *peso* did not buy much, but the loss was so important to us that my mother broke down and cried. The maid did not return, and we never recovered the money.

Near where we lived was a working class neighborhood. When I went to buy something at the corner grocery I observed how the poor did their own shopping. They bought what they needed by *centavos* or *pesos*, like one *peso* worth of sugar and fifty *centavos* worth of rice. It all depended on how much money they had. More often than not they had to buy on credit because they did not have enough cash to fill even minimal needs. Common staples were not boxed or prepackaged. The grocer would take the requested product out of a bag, box or barrel where it was stored and wrap it in a piece of paper, twirling the ends of the paper to make a tight little package. There were neither paper nor plastic shopping bags. It was pitiful to see how little these people carried away to feed their large families. A store around the corner sold wine. While the women did their shopping in the grocery store across the street, the men spent much of the family money (and sometimes all of it) on cheap wine. Chileans drank a lot of wine—red wine at lunch and at dinner. Children shared the mealtime wine from an early age. But the men also drank lots of wine between meals. This store was patronized by laborers who lived or worked in the neighborhood. The wine was of the cheapest quality and the customers brought their own containers in. They also drank it in the store illegally. At any hour of the day a constant stream of men went to a back room to drink wine right then and there. I was surprised that the cops, the *carabineros,* never bothered them, but I could guess. Often the policemen themselves went into the back room and came out a short while later wiping their lips.

At other times I shopped at a huge open air market a few blocks from where we lived. It was called the *Vega* and one could buy everything there: poultry, meat, vegetables, fish, fruit, flowers, household supplies and clothing. The walks between the stalls were narrow and crowded. When it rained the merchants strung sacks over the walks to protect themselves and their merchandise, but it did not help much. The market was dirty, and hygiene was not writ large. I felt sorry for the live chickens and ducks pressed together in open boxes like sardines in a can, expose⸺ ⸺ ⸺ ⸺ ⸺ ⸺ ⸺ to the rain, as they waited to be slaughtered. When it was hot, ⸺ ⸺ ith water to keep them from dying. The fruit 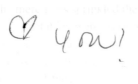 ⸺ vas the meat. I always sampled the tasty ch⸺ ⸺ stands that offered prepared foods, which w⸺ ⸺ lthough the prices were reasonable, I enga⸺ ⸺ ually successful in obtaining even lower pric⸺ ⸺ as this was the expected way of doing busine⸺

After a couple of years ⸺ neighborhood, where we lived in a small house with a fence in front and a garden in the back. Again, the largest room was reserved for the factory, which even after several years, still had the same cutting table and the same two sewing machines that we had relied on in the beginning. We still had no telephone. I could do my homework in the garden under the fruit trees surrounded by flowers. One of the trees was a *palto*, an avocado tree. In the evening I collected mint leaves, which grew wild among the flowers, and used them to make tea. One of the two seamstresses who had worked in the factory since the beginning lived in the maid's room at the rear of the garden. It was a wooden shack without any sanitary facilities. Summer or winter she had to cross the garden to use the maid's toilet and washroom located in an outdoor drafty wooden structure attached to the rear of the house. It was while we were living in this house that my parents passed through their hardest economic times. It was at this time that they bought the luncheonette with the thought that it would relieve their financial difficulties, but in fact, brought them even closer to financial ruin. They were tense from overwork, lack of sleep and constant, unrelenting worries. They squabbled frequently and would angrily shout at each other.

During one of these squabbles, after I had already gone to bed in my upstairs bedroom, I overheard my mother shout to my father in an irate voice that he had already put away one wife and was now intent on putting away the second. I wondered, "What was the meaning of that remark? Had there been a previous wife?" More important for me was the question, "Did I have any half-siblings that I didn't know about? If so, what had happened to them?" I asked my parents about my mother's comment the first thing in the morning. Their reply was that I had dreamed the whole thing, that there had been no previous marriage. I knew they were lying. I wanted to get to the bottom of this matter and started to investigate it, and soon made some progress. An old German custom was to engrave the inside of a wedding ring with the spouse's name and the wedding date. One day I saw my father's wedding ring lying on the night table, and I noticed that next to my mother's name there was another one together with a date that had been imperfectly obliterated. I was stunned by this discovery, which confirmed what I had overheard that night. My parents continued their steadfast denial for another year until finally my mother admitted the truth; my father had been married before. There had been, she said, no children from that marriage. She refused to tell me any more details of how my father had married his first wife in obedience to his mother, but against his will. The details I described earlier in this story regarding my grandmother I learned years later from two older cousins who witnessed the events.

One day in January of 1942, when I was in bed with jaundice and unable to go to the *Kidma*'s first summer camp, I heard that Ursel's mother had died at her own hand while her children were away at camp. She was no longer capable of accepting the deprivations of an immigrant's life. I knew no details other than that her husband found her unconscious when he came home in the evening, and that she had been rushed to a hospital where she died in spite of the doctor's attempt to save her. While she was in the hospital someone had gone to fetch the children from camp, but by the time they returned she was no longer alive. I was stunned by the news. It was the first time something like that had happened in my circle of friends. Our immigrant lives were harsh. Economic worries, concern about friends and relatives left behind in Germany and the loss of status affected all of our families. I frequently experienced the desperation of my parents and my friends, and knew that my parents were near the end of their physical and emotional resources. How desperate must Ursel's mother have been to have taken such a step—to leave her husband and teenage children to fend for themselves. Ursel was not my girlfriend at that time, but I liked her better than any other girl I knew. I was deeply moved when I heard the news and constantly thought of her. My first impulse was to rush out to be with her and console her, but of course I could not do that. I could not get out of bed and, in any event, I did not have a close relationship with her. My intrusion probably would have been inappropriate.

At the time, Ursel was not yet fourteen years old. With two exceptions, everybody in the close knit German-Jewish community knew how her mother had died. The exceptions were Ursel and her grandmother. We kept the information from them. The grandmother died without ever knowing the cause of her daughter's death. Ursel did not find out until she was nineteen, when her brother, in disbelief over her ignorance, told her. She was shocked. For five years she had believed that her mother had died from a fatal disease.

I was eleven when we arrived in Chile in November 1939. I was twenty-one when I left in 1949. I had gone to school, learned the language, associated with Chileans in my day-to-day affairs—but I never had a Chilean friend, never thought of myself as Chilean and never felt that I belonged to the country that had opened its doors to us when the need was greatest. During all these years I remained in our own small immigrant world—the world of the German-Jewish community. I had little interest in the country I called "home." Chile's history, culture, music, poets and people were of no concern. And I was not alone in this; it was a characteristic of the immigrant community, both among the young and old.

This separateness, this inability to be interested in my new environment even carried over into my contacts with Chilean Jews. In the Movement I associated with them, shared responsibilities and activities, but none of them ever became close friends. The boys who were my friends and the girls I fell in love with all had the same background; they were German Jews. Just like me, they were recent arrivals. Later, when we married it was the same. Most of us found partners within our small, tightly-knit immigrant community.

Later I reflected on the reasons for my limited outlook, for my refusal to enter into the culture of this new and different country. Why, I wondered, did I show such a lack of curiosity? Why so little exploration? I think this was partly due to the differing customs and habits of natives and newcomers. But for me, as for some of my friends, there were additional reasons that had to do with a planned future in which Chile would play no part.

Chileans welcomed, albeit sometimes grudgingly, the foreigners who had arrived as refugees. Earlier, other foreigners had been invited to come and fill the commercial, industrial, and military needs of the country. But Chileans did not generally mix with them. They tended to keep foreigners at a distance, and as a result most of the immigrants kept their distance as well. The result was not a multi-cultural society similar to what developed in the United States. Rather, it was a group of diverse separate societies and cultures living side by side, but never mixing. The children learned the attitudes of the adults in what proved to be a self-perpetuating cycle.

The policies of the Chilean government at that time did not help, but contributed to keeping the various communities apart. The law stated that immigrants could become citizens after five years in Chile. In practice, however, very few immigrants were granted citizenship during the 1940s. I knew only one person, my boss, who became a Chilean citizen, and that was through the influence of a powerful deputy in Congress who interceded on his behalf with the President of Chile.

For most of the newcomers, especially the older ones, the language was a great barrier, as was the burden of their past in Europe. These refugees had been forcibly expelled and deprived of all they had once valued: their country, their allegiance, their culture and their property. Unsettled in a new and strange land, they turned inward and wanted nothing so much as to recreate the life they had left behind and to regain what they had lost. There was no room for new experiences, at least not until much later when some of them learned the language. But many immigrants never succeeded in that.

This separateness carried over into all aspects of daily life. I sensed it everyday with the other children in school, it manifested itself in the clubs the foreign resident groups maintained (and still do), it showed in the social life that we carried on among members from our same group. It continues to this day. Many children of the old German Jewish community, who are the grandchildren of the original immigrants, attend a Jewish School and much of their social life takes place within the confines of the Jewish Club in Santiago. In 1996, a former immigrant who left Chile and had returned for a visit remarked on how separate, how enclosed, the German Jewish community in Chile still is—more than fifty years after the great World War II migration!

For me, as for my friends in the *Kidma*, there was another cause for the separateness we felt. Influenced by the *Kidma*, I was sure that Chile was a temporary home. I had larger goals that did not include Chile or Chileans. So it was only natural that I did not make an effort to enter the mainstream society. My goal was to build a Jewish homeland in Palestine, and within that homeland, a better society as exemplified by the *kibbutz*. I never verbalized these thoughts. They were simply there, self-understood and ever-present.

As I grew older, my horizons broadened and I discovered music, books and theater. When I was fourteen, my father bought our first radio—a beautiful jewel that played music at the push of a button. The first music I heard when I turned it on the first time was a toccata by Frescobaldi. I was so impressed that I never forgot it and can still whistle the main melody, although it is seldom played anymore. My next musical discovery was a performance of Beethoven's Ninth Symphony. It was performed in a sports arena near the center of town normally dedicated to wrestling matches. Called the *Teatro Caupolicán*, it was named after a 16th century Araucano Indian who resisted the Spanish conquest of Chile. I took little interest in the first three movements waiting impatiently for the last, the choral "Ode to Joy," *Freude, schöner Götterfunken* (Joy, radiant spark of the Gods), set to a poem by the German poet Schiller, which I knew from the radio.

There followed my first opera, Leoncavallo's "Pagliacci" performed in Santiago's beautiful, plush opera house, the *Teatro Municipal*. I listened to a radio transmission of Wagner's opera "Tannhäuser" one afternoon when I visited Ursel at her home. A violinist with the unusual name of Yehudi Menuhin played, in the *Teatro Municipal*, music by a composer named Bartok whose name I had never heard before, music that in the 1940s sounded strange to me. With these first tentative steps, followed by more concerts and operas in the *Teatro Municipal*, on the radio and on records, I had discovered one of the great passions of my life.

In 1944 at the age of sixteen, I became the editor of the Movement's news bulletin. I thought it would be a great idea to take advantage of Yehudi Menuhin's presence in Santiago to interview him. I wanted to ask him some simple questions about Zionism and the future of the Jewish state in Palestine. After all, I reasoned, a famous Jewish man should know about such matters. After an evening concert I followed the violinist to his hotel, the *Carrera*, the best in town. At the desk I asked for Menuhin's room number, but the concierge, rightly, would not tell me. I was lucky. A distinguished looking man came in and requested the same information. He was given the room number. I overheard it. I went up to the room, entered, and there, facing the door, was the great man, relaxing in an armchair with a drink in his hand. He was flanked by two other men standing beside the chair like bodyguards. I quickly approached and in my faulty English asked the key question on my mind: what did he think of the "bi-national state in Palestine?" Just as quickly one of the men standing next to the chair grabbed this intruder, me, by the collar of his shirt and threw him out. Thus ended my interview.

Then there were books. I discovered German authors such as Stefan Zweig, Franz Werfel and Thomas Mann and poems by Goethe, Schiller and Heine. I struggled through Pearl Buck's "The Good Earth," in English. It opened an exotic view of China. In Spanish I read Cervantes' "*Don* Quijote." But I only read one book by a Chilean author, a romantic novel titled "Martín Rivas" written at the end of the previous century by Alberto Blest Gana. The book touched me with its subject matter, which involved a romance where love overcame all obstacles presented by a girl's wealth and a boy's poverty. It was like a fairy tale, a wonderful dream. I projected myself into that boy's place and dreamed of a beautiful girl who would pull me out of poverty and provide me with romance. The book left a deep impression on me, precisely because of my own circumstances. I always remembered it, even after I had long forgotten the title and the author. I also read the early love poems by Pablo Neruda, which vividly spoke to my awakening romantic yearnings, and a few poems by Gabriela Mistral. She "did not speak to me," however, as Neruda did, although both of these Chilean poets later won the Nobel Prize for Literature. My reading was random and lacking guidance, but it was a good beginning. I had found the second great passion of my life.

I also saw a lot of movies. There was a movie theater near our house, and I made the acquaintance of a couple of ushers. When I wanted to go to the movies, I walked the few blocks to the theater, slipped a small tip to the usher on duty and went in. The movies I saw in this neighborhood theater were not great, but they were fun. I remember one about San Francisco, where the earth shook while Jeanette MacDonald sang beautiful songs. In another titled "Blood and Sand," which was about bullfights, Rita Hayworth stole the spotlight from the bulls. A pity, because the bullfighting in the movie was pretty good. "Dr. Jekyll and Mr. Hyde" was scary. I wondered how Spencer Tracy could change his face the way he did with the camera focused on him.

Some movies were not shown in the neighborhood theater. I had to see them in the center of town at the regular price. They left deep impressions. A new film in spectacular color, "Gone with the Wind," showed an epic of the American civil war. It was romantic, not true to history, but that did not matter. It was glorious. I watched it sitting in the plush seat of Santiago's most expensive movie house at a ticket price I could hardly afford. "The Great Waltz," the life of Johann Strauss, with its rendition of the "Tales from the Vienna Woods" and "Blue Danube" was unforgettable. I admired pretty Teresa Wright in "Mrs. Miniver," which was about a heroic English family at the time of the evacuation of the British Expeditionary Forces from Dunkirk during the Second World War. "For Whom the Bell Tolls," a romantic story about the Spanish civil war with Ingrid Bergman, who so resembled Ursel, introduced me to Hemingway. And a film with the violinist Jasha Heifetz converted me forever into a devotee of the great violinist. What all these films had in common was that they provided an escape. For a few hours I immersed myself in the lives of other people in other places, in beautiful music and exciting dramas. During that time I could forget the cares of home, the pressures of the Movement and anything else that was worrying me.

There was one horrifying exception. After the war in Europe was over and the extermination camps opened, a film was shown in one of the Santiago theaters about the atrocities committed by the Germans. I went to see it and was shocked by the images of the surviving, emaciated prisoners; the thousands of skeletons of the murdered; the mass graves; gas ovens and crematoria. It was unimaginable how this could have happened. I knew no words that would vent my feelings of rage, sadness and horror. I knew that friends and relatives left behind after our departure from Germany were among the victims. Later I saw these images again and again, and I never got used to them. But that first time, when the images were fresh, overshadowed anything I saw in the future.

I also took some tentative steps into the world of theater. In the *Teatro Municipal,* Thornton Wilder's "Our Town," performed by the University of Chile's Experimental Theater, moved me to tears (and still does), but in Pirandello's play I did not understand why those six characters were in search of an author (and I still don't). The first time I saw "Hamlet" was in a Yiddish performance. I understood just enough of the language to follow the action. For some reason I found the soliloquy "To be or not to be" in Yiddish funny. It was at the *Teatro Municipal* that I saw my first ballet, Delibes' "Cóppelia." The lovely performance remains a treasured memory.

Before I had a job I was always short of spending money. There were two ways to stretch what I had. One was to earn more money. The other was to make what I had go further. To earn money, I did odd jobs for neighbors and friends. A law required ground floor residents of an apartment building to sweep the sidewalk in front of the building. I did that for our own house when we lived on the ground floor and then got paid to do the neighboring house. I bought household items from wholesalers at the Vega such as soap, toothpaste, toilet paper and cleansers, and then resold them to my parents and acquaintances at a small profit. To stretch what I had, I handed the ushers tips instead of buying tickets to gain entrance to a theater. This worked not only in the neighborhood movie houses but also for concerts and operas in the *Teatro Municipal.* Returning tickets on streetcars and busses and then obtaining an occasional free ride was yet another way of stretching what I had.

One day I had entered the *Teatro Municipal* by the stage door, climbed up to the rafters from which the scenery hung, and sat down on one of the walkways to watch the performance on the stage below. It was Verdi's "Otello," and I blissfully listened to Desdemona, dangling my legs as she sang her prayers in the last act just before she is strangled by Otello. Suddenly, I was roughly pulled up by a strange man who had been sent to investigate the source of shadows moving across poor Desdemona as she was absorbed in preparing for her death. The darting shadows came from my moving legs. In no time I was on the street, resenting the abrupt interruption of my enjoyment of that heavenly music.

Paintings, sculpture and architecture were out of my reach. Chile had little to offer and the reproductions available in books only gave a hint of the great works that existed elsewhere. Later, in museums all over the world, I had the opportunity to see originals of the great masters and this added to my list of passions.

Life Within the Family

My relations with my family continued to be difficult. My parents worked so hard that they had little time for me. They put food on the table, albeit modest and not always enough, and they took care of my health as best they could. They provided shelter and clothing. They found time to arrange for my *Bar Mitzvah* and the lessons leading up to it, and my father arranged my first job and went with me to buy my first pair of long pants and suit. What was lacking was any sort of emotional closeness. Although this was partly due to their preoccupation with making a living, I believe that a more important reason was their inability to understand the needs of their teenage son. This continued the pattern they had established in Germany, where my daily upbringing had been left to the maid. In addition there was the matter of age. When I had my *Bar Mitzvah*, my father was already fifty-seven and my mother fifty-five. In those years, this was an unusually large age difference between parents and children. Perhaps more important than the age difference was that they had been born and brought up at the end of the preceding century, with the rigid moral and behavioral standards of that time. Those standards admitted no deviation. My parents never accepted the changes that came during the 20th century. They never grew in that respect. They were old-fashioned and remained that way. My perception was that my parents were too old to understand me. The gulf between their ideas and mine was great, and I perceived them as grandparents rather than as parents.

I became independent very early. At twelve I had a key to the house and rarely bothered to tell anyone where I was going or when I would be home. I went to school and did my homework. I was always there when my father needed help with his business. Yet I considered my free time my own. My parents, in turn, thought of me as misbehaved. I often had fights with them, and more often with my mother than with my father. I can no longer recall what brought on the constant fights, only that they always ended in tears and resentment.

What I did with my free time was innocent enough. Some of it I spent with activities related to the *Kidma*. Sometimes I went to the movies. In summer an activity took place in the center of Santiago to which I returned frequently. This center was the *Plaza de Armas* (the Weapons Square). It was surrounded by an 18th century cathedral, the main post office and commercial galleries with many different kinds of shops. Every evening boys and girls, men and women, circulated around the lawns and flowers and the bandstand in the center of the square, with the men going one way and women the other in two concentric circles. They smiled at each other without speaking. Perhaps they were looking for company for the evening, for the night or for life. It was an age old ritual of Spanish origin, repeated over and over in similar squares in towns all over South America. I liked to join the fun, going round and round with the others, even if I never smiled at the girls. I was too shy and felt inhibited. This ritual lasted an hour or more, and when the fun was over, I crossed the street to one of the galleries. At an open stand I could buy an *empanada,* a mixture of meat, olives, eggs and spices in a baked crust, which was a tasty Chilean specialty that was my favorite. Or I would eat a hot dog or hamburger covered with sauerkraut and smothered by mayonnaise and mustard.

On weekends I often went up a 1,000-foot mountain, the San Cristóbal, which rose north of Santiago on the opposite side of the Mapocho River. Alone and with friends I'd climb one of the many footpaths leading to the top, or sometimes, just for fun, I'd ride the funicular, a cable car which got its passengers to the top in less than five minutes. The first thing that greeted a visitor was the 120-foot statue of the Virgin Mary, which was tall enough to contain a chapel in its pedestal. No matter when I went up there, day or evening, I'd find a constant stream of the faithful who had come to the chapel to kneel and pray. The view from here of the city and the snowy mountains beyond was overwhelming. Down in Santiago the resplendently white statue could be seen from many different places in the city, and it dominated the landscape. Seen from the center of town, the mountain looked isolated, as if it stood alone. In fact, in the back it stretched for miles. I have special memories of the San Cristóbal. It never snows in Santiago, or almost never, but during the winter months the surrounding mountains are always covered with snow. On one rare day in 1941, it did snow in the city, which caused quite a sensation. I looked out the window in the morning, saw the snow, and without telling anyone decided I would cut school that day. I dressed, not very well for that kind of weather, and as quickly as possible hiked up the mountain. I played in the snow, which I had not seen or touched since leaving Europe. Then, I decided to bring some snow back down with me. I made a big snow ball, as big as I could carry and lugged it to our apartment. The ball was so big that when I put it in the patio it did not melt for days.

On another day there was a total eclipse of the sun. Up on the mountain, a mile or so from the statue, was an astronomical observatory. On the morning of the eclipse, Ursel and I climbed to the observatory and watched as the city slowly went dark, as if night had fallen in the middle of the day, and then we watched as little by little the city returned to its normal daylight self. Some press photographer took a picture of the spectators, and the next day we saw ourselves in a newspaper photo.

My parents tried to borrow money to transfer the two *Lifts* that had been sent from Königsberg to Rotterdam in the Netherlands for temporary storage. Their contents would have been more than enough to repay the borrowed money. But they were not successful. Later they were notified by a Dutch company that the *Lifts* had been destroyed. Whether they had been destroyed by the Germans during the bombing of Rotterdam or whether they had been pilfered we never learned. Many years later two golden watches from the *Lifts* arrived in our home, mysteriously, with no indication of who had sent them or how they had found their way to us. They were watches that had been given to my brother and me by our cousin Lola as mementos before she left for Israel in the mid-thirties. My parents had smuggled them into the *Lifts* when they had packed them in Königsberg. They were old fashioned and no longer worked, but they represented a cherished memory and I have kept my watch to this day.

My father's health was a constant concern. When he was sick there was no one else who was capable of conducting the external aspects of the business: selling, taking orders, buying materials, collecting payments due, dealing with the banks that had extended credits on the notes we received in payment for merchandise. Our doctors, like those of most other immigrants, were German-speaking immigrant physicians. Immigrant doctors were unlicensed. The Chilean government, under pressure from local doctors who feared the competition, refused to grant them professional licenses. Some of these doctors had been eminent physicians in Germany. In spite of being unlicensed, several were called to treat VIP Chileans, including the President of the Republic. For immigrants they performed a vital function. My parents were unable to speak the language and could not have explained their symptoms to a Chilean doctor. The immigrant physicians understood them and could treat them. Ursel's father was such a doctor. But he was unwilling to work illegally as a physician and had a hard time earning a living.

Not all these doctors were competent. One day in the winter of 1941, my father did not feel well and it soon became apparent that he was seriously ill. We called one of the unlicensed immigrant doctors. My father got sicker and sicker under his care. Desperate, my mother arranged to have my father admitted to a hospital, where we learned that the doctor had treated him for pneumonia when, in fact, he had typhus. Once the right diagnosis was made, he improved, but remained weak for a long time.

One day when my father was sixty, he came home with severe chest pains. He often had suffered such pains, which had first begun to afflict him six years earlier while we were still living in Germany. He had been diagnosed as having angina, a coronary heart disease that reduces blood flow to the heart, and he was given nitroglycerin to relieve the pain. The pills usually helped. But on this occasion it was different. The pain was severe and the nitroglycerin failed to offer any relief. A doctor was called and he saw that my father had suffered a heart attack. It was his first one. Father stayed in bed for a while and then went back to work. But the writing was on the wall. We were aware that his condition was serious, more serious than anything that he had suffered previously. There was nothing to prevent a recurrence. My mother and I were worried. Although Father did not say anything about it, I sensed that he was worried too. When he started talking about bringing in a partner for the business, I realized that he was aware of the threat to himself and to his family. He did not need to verbalize his fears. A few months later there was a recurrence—and then there was another and another and another. In all, he had five heart attacks in three years. The fifth one killed him.

We had moved from the house to an apartment, and the factory had been relocated in the center of town. This was the first time since we had come to Chile that we lived in a home that did not serve simultaneously as a factory. Even so, to make ends meet, my parents had to rent out one of the three bedrooms. We still had no telephone.

On the final night of my father's life, a Friday evening, I was sitting in the living room reading a book. My father had gone to bed around midnight. He came out half-an-hour later complaining that he could not get any air, that he could not breathe. He said something to me he had never said during any of his previous attacks. He said, "Siegfried, this is the end." He sat down. My mother came to help him and I raced out to find a telephone so I could call the doctor. The apartment was close to a working class neighborhood that included bars, cheap eating places and a red light district. I found a telephone in an open bar and got through to the doctor. He arrived at our apartment within a half-hour. My father was lying on the couch, still alive and conscious, but his face had turned blue and he was slowly asphyxiating. The doctor's ministrations were unsuccessful. My father lapsed into unconsciousness after a few minutes and died at 1:00 a.m. on Saturday morning. His statement to me had been prophetic. The date was August 30, 1947. He was a month short of his sixty-third birthday. When I saw his body stretched out on the sofa hidden by a sheet, I slowly grasped that I would never be able to speak to him again, or seek his help or advice as I had done on so many previous occasions. The loss cut deep as it sank in. Soon the apartment began to fill up. My brother arrived with his new wife and her father, who was also a doctor. Our maid of many years arrived in the morning and was stunned. She, like many others who worked for him, had liked my kind father. Friends came. I could not stand it in the apartment and did something that can only be considered irrational. In the morning I went downtown to keep a dental appointment. The dentist was a friend, a member of the *Kidma,* and it took some time for me to tell him that a few hours earlier my father had died. He did not say much beyond expressing his sympathy, but he must have been surprised at my being there. At the end of the Sabbath the hearse arrived to transport the body to the cemetery. As religious custom required, my brother and I walked with the hearse for a block before it took off at its normal speed and we returned home. He was buried a couple of days later at the Jewish cemetery in Santiago.

The factory continued to operate without him for a few more years. My mother and the partner saw to that, but the driving force and energy that my father provided were gone. Henceforth, the business seemed sad and tired. When I stopped by it seemed to me that the activities were performed in a spiritless way without much enthusiasm.

When my father died I was nineteen, which was not old enough to have known him as an adult. I loved my father. I enjoyed his company during the rare moments when we were together and I always regretted that he died before I got to know him well.

Education...or the Lack of It

Growing up in Santiago, my main concerns were my education, the choice of a profession, the Movement and, naturally, girls. I obtained only a limited formal education, chose a profession that ultimately led to a professional career, was a faithful member of the Movement until I rebelled against it and I found the girl I loved and would marry before I left Chile in another emigration.

I spoke no Spanish when I arrived in Chile. True, there had been Spanish lessons during my final months in Hamburg, but what I learned was negligible. Shortly after our arrival in Santiago, my parents sent me to a Spanish language course in the Jewish School, the *Instituto Hebreo.* The course lasted only a few weeks, and the result was once again negligible. But I was so ambitious and self-confident, so cocky, that I applied to be admitted to the prestigious elite high school, the *Instituto Nacional.* I went to the examination knowing little Spanish, no Chilean history, and none of the subject matter that had been taught in the lower grades up to that point. At the exam I could not even understand the questions, let alone answer them. It was an effort preordained to failure, and I failed.

My next attempt at learning the language came through private lessons. A private teacher tried to drum the language into my head by rote exercises. The teacher was an old man. During the lessons we sat on the hot patio of our first apartment and the teacher frequently nodded off. He taught me some grammar, but not how to apply it, and he did not teach me how to speak the language. After several weeks the lessons were terminated.

It was now time for me to go to a regular school. The school year began at the end of summer in March. In 1940, the Chilean school system was divided into preparatory grades, the *preparatorias,* which were followed by high school, the *humanidades,* each of which lasted six years. There was no coeducation. Public schools were either for boys or for girls. I always went to school in my normal street clothes, but the girls wore uniforms. It was a no-nonsense school system, with a heavy emphasis on the three "R's": reading, writing and arithmetic. We were taught with little imagination or innovation. Most of the teachers had probably never heard of "modern" teaching methods. Also taught were singing, sports and religion—Catholic religion. Like other Jewish children, I was excused from the religious classes, which were conducted by priests. Some of the Jewish students did attend these classes, either because they were curious or because they were attracted to Catholicism. I never did. The schools were old, and so were the desks, chairs and tables. But notwithstanding the primitive surroundings, we learned our lessons and nobody was advanced to higher grades without passing the required final examinations at the end of each grade. We had a one-week break between the last day of classes and the examinations, which we used to prepare ourselves for the tests. To study for the tests I often went to the *Cerro* Santa Lucía.

The *Cerro* Santa Lucía, a 300-foot hill, rose near the center of town alongside the main, east-west avenue. It was completely covered, top to bottom, with lush tropical vegetation. On the top were fortifications dating back to colonial times. I often climbed up to the highest point, a lookout that contained an ancient canon that was fired every day at noon. It was a blank round that was heard many blocks away. Everybody who heard it, including me, stopped what they were doing at that moment to check their watches. When I was there at noon, I watched as two men loaded the cannon, and at a signal from one, the other fired the shot. It never failed, or almost never. Every time I went up I followed a different path. The wider, more open paths were interrupted by little plazas with benches, where I passed mothers watching their small children, school children doing homework or studying for their examinations, and others who were reading books or just idling their time away. I passed a laboratory where seismographs monitored the innumerable earthquakes that constantly shook the country. Sometimes I went up one of the more secluded paths that young couples liked for their walks. In the evening, the hill welcomed other couples, or perhaps the same ones, who needed darkness for their love, as well as strollers seeking relaxation and peace after the day's tasks were accomplished. Their peace was occasionally interrupted by robbers who sought out the darkness for more sinister purposes. During most breaks as long as I went to school, I carried my books to the Santa Lucía and found my favorite secluded corner, a rock overlooking the Catholic University below and the snow capped mountains beyond. It was there that I studied for the exams. It was so peaceful that I sometimes just sat and daydreamed. But I mostly studied and always passed my examinations with flying colors.

When I first started school, I was old enough to be able to enter the seventh school year, the first year of *humanidades*. But my lack of Spanish language knowledge posed an insurmountable barrier. Instead, my parents found a grade school some distance away, the *Liceo de Aplicación*, where one of the fifth grade teachers who spoke a little German was willing to accept immigrant children in his class and help them with their language problems. That was where I went. It could not have been a more pleasant, positive experience, due to the caring, considerate and sympathetic attitude of the teacher.

Senõr Hernández, Luis Hernández, was a wizened little old man, with gray hair and eyebrows an inch long, who was so old fashioned in his attire that he looked almost absurd. There were five immigrant children in his class. He cared for us as a mother hen would for her chicks. The class was conducted in Spanish, but at critical moments he would take time out to translate words and phrases. In this way, little by little, almost without noticing it, I learned Spanish. By the end of the school year, few if any translations were needed. He made the Chilean children understand the immigrants' situation, and he exhorted them to be friendly and helpful. Fortunately, they were. They were kind and curious all through that school year. I have a picture that shows my fifth grade class of 1940. Fifty-seven years later I can pick out certain children and remember their names.

Of course not everything was easy and there were students in the school who were not so understanding. A particularly unpleasant experience was related to the pants I wore. Even at that age, Chilean children wore long pants, but I did not have any. I had German training pants used for sports, that looked like long jogging pants but without a fly. Those were the pants that I wore to school. The children made fun of me and laughed because I was wearing *calzones* (women's panties). People laughed at me on my way to school, on the streetcar and on the bus. I was ashamed but did not understand why they were laughing. It took me some time to figure it out. When I did, I refused to wear those pants ever again. But my parents didn't have any money to buy me a pair of long pants, so all through that winter I wore shorts to school and I was cold.

Señor Hernández did not limit his care to the school and classroom. He invited his "special" children to the tearoom at the city's most fashionable department store. He often picked us up and delivered us back home by taxi. I had not seen surroundings like these and had not been served in such a gracious manner since the signs had gone up outside German cafes refusing admittance to Jews. I had never tasted food like this either—little sandwiches and cakes served on elegant china. On these occasions, *Señor* Hernández would draw us out and take an obvious interest in our thoughts, experiences and families. He was full of compassion and helped us in whatever way he could. After he found out about my violin lessons in Germany but that I could not afford to buy a violin here, he provided me with one that he owned but did not use. I made good use of it, practicing a little and playing in the youth orchestra of the Movement. I took unfair advantage of my teacher's kindness and never returned the violin. I have felt guilty about that ever since.

Señor Hernández lived by himself in one or two rooms in an old Chilean house called a *conventillo*, a tenement house. Similar to what I had seen when I visited our seamstresses, the house consisted of a number of one story high dwelling units around a large common patio. But these units had running water and indoor toilets, and were a step above the dwellings occupied by the poorer working class. His rooms were cluttered from top to bottom with all sorts of gadgets he had collected, and the violin was one of them.

I was too young at the age of twelve to inquire about the teacher's life. Why was he so alone? Had he ever been married? Did he have any children? What caused him to show such care and sympathy for us? I rarely saw him after that year in his class, and by the time I was old enough to begin asking myself such questions, he had died. I never again met a person like *Señor* Hernández.

My second year at school brought a separation from my benevolent mentor and the nurturing environment he provided. Having learned the language, I transferred to a neighborhood school within walking distance from our apartment. I was now in the sixth preparatory grade, still two years behind where I should have been. I was a good student. We had the same teacher for all subjects. Teaching was by rote. I memorized the names of all the lakes of a given country, or all the mountains or provinces. It was the same method for all the subjects taught, whether mathematics, history or grammar. I was also taught one extracurricular lesson in this class. Chilean schoolboys had a habit of challenging each other to a fight, for no particular reason other than to fight. One day I was walking home with a classmate who suddenly asked me whether I wanted to fight. I did not understand the intent of the question and considered it a joke. I agreed, whereupon he put down his books, and with his fist landed a tremendous blow square on my face, breaking my nose. Then he left as if nothing had happened. I was bleeding heavily and a passerby called an ambulance to take me to the hospital. There the attendant stopped the bleeding and the doctor set the nose, which he left crooked. Later in the day my father took me to a private doctor to have my nose reset. He did a poor job too, and my nose has never looked straight since. The next day when I went back to school, the boy who had punched me expressed no interest in what had happened and I did not tell him. But I never again accepted a challenge from any of my classmates to fight. I had learned my lesson.

When the school year was over, I was ready to enroll in the high school, the *liceo,* for the first year of *humanidades*. Now there was a different teacher for each subject, including the foreign language of English. Generally school now was a more interesting place. Here, too, I was a good student. There were several other immigrant children in my class. Surprisingly I excelled in Spanish grammar and received better grades than the Chilean students. I had no contact with my Chilean co-students in the school or outside of it. I never visited them in their homes, nor did I ever invite them to mine. This pattern did not change during the next school year, which was my last one.

I was troubled by being two school years behind and decided to try to skip the next grade. I studied all summer with the help of an older boy who was also an immigrant. I almost wore out my study rock on the Santa Lucía. My reward was complete success in the required examinations, even in French, which was another new language for me. Then the school, under some pretext I did not understand, denied me admission to the next grade. I almost broke down and cried out of sheer frustration. After strenuous negotiations I succeeded in having that decision reversed and I entered the third year of *humanidades*. It was to be my last year of public school in Chile. In 1943, at age fifteen, I quit school to seek work.

By 1943 my parents had sufficient income for me to have stayed in school. In fact, at the beginning of the school year I had thought of continuing in school, my grades were good and education was important to me. But as the year wore on, little by little I gave up that idea. An entry in my diary dated November 27, 1943, records that the school year had provided me with little satisfaction and that I was not sorry to leave. But only three weeks later the diary records the exact opposite, that I regretted leaving school. Apparently, my regret was not strong enough to reverse my decision.

I had been eager to obtain an education and attend the university. I had planned on becoming an engineer. I had even picked out the university, which was in Valparaiso and provided scholarships for capable students in need. Then somehow my mind went blank. I dropped this idea. How did that happen?

By now, I had come completely under the influence of the Movement and the idea that Palestine needed proletarian workers had taken hold. For that, a university education was unnecessary. I accepted and believed the Movement's dogma. It was as if resolute brainwashing had erased all memory of my previous plans. This was reinforced by my closest friends, who left school at about the same time. All were members of my group in the Movement, all my age, so it seemed natural that I should do likewise. At fifteen I was too young to perceive how detrimental this misguided decision was.

There was no role model for me to emulate that could have countered the Movement's influence. In my family, nobody had ever gone to a university. This was true of my parents who did not even attempt to advise me to stay in school. Had they tried, I probably would not have listened to them anyway. There was nobody else—no family friend, no teacher, nor a mentor outside the *Kidma* who tried to reverse my decision. Years later, when I did earn a university degree, I was the first ever in my family to do so.

Leaving public school was not quite the end of my education. There followed two periods of vocational schools. The first was in a school established by a Jewish organization called ORT, which stood for Organization for Rehabilitation through Training. The purpose of the school was to train students to become mechanics. The curriculum was designed to last for two or three years. I did not like the school and felt misplaced. I rebelled against the teaching of Spanish as part of the curriculum and refused to attend Spanish classes. But even the technical classes turned me off. I could not produce mechanical drawings, could not do the work in the shop, could not handle the tools and did not care about properties of materials. It was hopeless. After a few months I left ORT and felt liberated.

Things were different at my next vocational school. By that time I had become a radio technician and enrolled in a five-month course to study the subject matter. This time I was fascinated by what I learned about vacuum tubes and electromagnetic waves, about sound and how it was produced and how radios worked and why they sometimes did not. From then on I used every opportunity to expand what I learned at school. This modest beginning determined my future professional life and led me to my chosen career. After I finished the vocational course, I followed it up with private lessons, taking classes from an engineer who taught me algebra, trigonometry, physics and electronics. This was my last professional training in Chile.

Earning a Living

My brother went to work almost immediately after our arrival in Santiago. The small wages he earned as an apprentice car mechanic were needed to help support us. He was fourteen-and-a-half, and he had finished less that nine years of school. He never spoke to me about how he felt about his situation, but he was not alone. Many immigrant children his age, boys and girls alike, started to work as soon as they arrived. I was luckier. Since I was three years younger, I was able to go to school for a little while longer.

After leaving school, it was my turn to look for work. I was not sure what I wanted to do, but I had a vague idea that I'd like to work in a shop that built or repaired electric equipment. I was willing to explore other technical work. But I did not want to go into sales or do office work. I had several interviews, but received no job offers.

In the meantime, I continued to assist in the factory: helping my father in his sales efforts, packing and delivering merchandise, translating when my father's language skills were insufficient. I disliked the work but had no other choice.

In the end it was my father who arranged for my first job. An acquaintance was a co-owner of a factory for small electric parts: switches, wall outlets and the like. In his factory, huge machines stamped out components that had to be assembled into finished products. To produce each component, precise hand-made steel tools were attached to the machines. I was hired as an apprentice toolmaker to produce these tools. I started work the first week of May 1944, two weeks short of my sixteenth birthday.

I had never experienced facilities as primitive as those provided to the workers in this factory. Although it was winter, there was little or no heat. Dirty washrooms had only cold water faucets and lacked soap. There was no place to eat lunch. The workers ate the hot lunches brought by their wives to the factory in special food carriers at their benches. All this was similar to other Chilean factories at that time. It was merely an extension of the poor conditions existing in the workers' homes. But to me, accustomed to the European standards generally maintained in immigrant homes, this was a shock. I experienced a second shock when I discovered that I completely lacked the aptitude for this work.

As an apprentice, I was paid minimal wages and was not expected to "produce"—at least not in the beginning. On my first day, the mechanic assigned as my mentor gave me a block of metal and told me to cut and file it to produce a cube, two inches to each side. By definition, a cube needs to have six equal faces at right angles to each other. After I cut the metal to an approximate size I started to file. I filed, and I filed, and I filed, and at no point was I able to produce sides that stood at right angles. The cube became two inches, and then shrank to one-and-three-quarters, and then to one-and-a-half inches—and then I quit. Five weeks of this torture had gone by. I walked over to the office and gave one week's notice. The supervisor fired me on the spot, with an extra week of pay thrown in as required by law. I said good-bye to the owners. One of them called me ungrateful, showing no understanding of this confused inexperienced teenager who had discovered something about himself he had not known before. The other owner just wished me good luck in whatever profession I chose. I left without regrets.

When I came home with my first week's pay, Mother demanded that I hand over the money so she could administer it and give me an allowance. It was similar to the agreement she had with my brother. I refused. I gave her an allowance for the household and managed the rest by myself. It was my final step toward independence.

Leaving my first job was no loss. While I had been filing my misshapen block of metal, a letter arrived at home offering me a job as a radio technician. I did not want to make another mistake, so I thought long and hard before I accepted. However, the Movement once again tried to intervene. The issue was whether a radio technician would be useful in a *kibbutz*. I consulted with one of the leaders, who was six years older, about what I should do. He advised me not to accept the job because he was absolutely certain, so he said, it would have no application in the *kibbutz*. Only mechanics were needed there! For once my commonsense prevailed over an uninformed opinion. I rejected his advice, became a radio technician and stayed happily on that job for four years, until the owner closed the shop so that he could seek greener pastures in America.

The business was located in the center of town. It was small. It sold new and used radios and had a shop that repaired radios and other electronic equipment. It was called *Taller Electrón*. Peter, the owner and manager, was a skilled technician, and he had hired two additional technicians and a *mozo*. I was one of the technicians. I liked the work and was convinced that I had chosen the right profession. Back then, radios used vacuum tubes as transistors had not been yet invented. Printed circuits were also unheard of, and individual wires had to be soldered to contacts to establish electric connections. When I soldered the wires, it did not matter how round or square the joint was as long as it was solid. I had no problem with that. When a radio was brought in that was silent, or hoarse, or noisy, I felt like a doctor. I used complicated instruments to establish a diagnosis for the radio's illness and then proceeded to cure it. Often a great deal of ingenuity was required to find a cure. Some radios were old, going back to the 1920s when the very first radios had been made. Replacement parts no longer existed. Other radios had been manufactured in Europe, and due to the war time conditions, tubes and components were not available in Chile. Replacement parts for American radios were also often in short supply. So I had to invent ingenious methods to make the repairs. I enjoyed doing that. It presented a challenge. When successful, I felt a sense of pride and accomplishment.

I repaired radios, movie projectors, medical equipment and hearing aids that were heavy and bulky and were worn on the belt of the user. I also repaired record players. They played heavy, twelve-inch records with about four minutes of music on each side. Longer musical works, like a symphony, required seven or eight records. More than 100 records would have been needed to play Richard Wagner's *"Der Ring des Nibelungen"*—a series of four operas that lasted fourteen hours. Nobody had ever attempted to record something that ambitious.

One time in 1948, a customer brought in something new for repair. It was a machine that could be used to record voices or music on a magnetized wire that ran from a spool on one side of the recorder to a spool on the other. I recorded the major part of an opera transmission from the *Teatro Municipal* on this marvel. The "Ring" had just shrunk from a hundred records to a few spools of wire. I did not repair television sets. Although I had seen a black-and-white TV demonstration in Königsberg in 1936, television was not yet in commercial use. Instead, people used movie projectors and owned films. They were mostly silent, but a few wealthier people owned sound projectors and films.

The movie projectors provided me with a profitable sideline of work. For extra pay I showed movies at children's birthday parties in well-to-do homes, mostly on evenings and weekends. I entertained the children by showing them cartoon and slapstick movies. I often got tips in addition to my pay. Sometimes the hosts offered me something to eat. On those occasions, I was served in the kitchen together with the servants. Even so, I enjoyed the food. I saw how the wealthy lived in their well-kept houses, with gardens tended by gardeners, and their ample kitchens where cooks prepared the abundant food for the hosts and guests, all dressed up in elegant clothes. It was all so different from the way my parent's seamstresses lived; so different from the way I lived. One time I showed movies in the residence of the owner of Chile's most important newspaper, *El Mercurio*. The show was put on in the basement of the residence. At the touch of a button, a screen came down from the ceiling and a projector came out of a hidden place in the wall. Electric trains were running in and out of walls all around the room. I was impressed. I felt envious! I thought that this lifestyle was inaccessible, forever closed to me. Although at this time my goals were still directed toward Palestine and the *kibbutz*, these situations made me think about whether I really wanted to live the life envisioned for Palestine, or whether I would be happier outside the Movement, finding my own way in life. These thoughts entered into my considerations when the time came for me to decide my future.

Around 1946 my boss, Peter, acquired a car. Few people could afford one. Peter's car was a 1928 two-seater Ford. It was a proud moment when he drove it for the first time and invited me out for a ride. I often accompanied him on deliveries or service calls he made in the car. One day on a busy street in the middle of town, a wheel fell off. The car could not be repaired and was replaced with a newer 1932 model.

Every year on the anniversary of the shop's founding, Peter invited his two technicians to dinner in one of Santiago's fancy restaurants. I was always hungry and was not used to good food, so I sometimes ate two dinners on these occasions, much to the amusement of Peter and the other technician. Over time, Peter became much more than a boss. He was a mentor, advisor and a friend who had a decisive influence on my life. He helped to broaden my horizons in unexpected ways. Peter introduced me to new music that I did not know, for example Lalo's and Paganini's violin concertos and Wagner's opera "Meistersinger." In this opera I listened to ugly and grotesque singing and could not believe that a famous composer had written it. I was aghast. Peter patiently explained that it was done on purpose, that a character named Beckmesser sang this way to highlight the beautiful melodies that were sung by the hero. It was my first lesson on how operas could be written to convey the composer's ideas and meanings.

During one of his vacations, Peter visited the Inca ruins of Machu Picchu in Peru. His account of the ruins and the ancient Inca culture left me no peace until I was able to visit them myself decades later. He introduced me to new ideas about world government and world peace that were far removed from the class struggle I had been taught about in the Movement. He provided a healthy and much needed antidote to the militant dogma and ideology in which I had been immersed. Acting as a catalyst, he made me see the Movement's ideas in a new and different light that, eventually, caused me to reject them. We were considering becoming partners using a cash infusion into the shop from my father, but before that could happen, my father died and both Peter and I made other plans.

Life in the Movement... from Commitment to Rebellion

After the *Kidma* became the *Hashomer Hatzaïr* in 1943, I accepted the new goals without questioning them. I was a committed member who enthusiastically participated in all activities and firmly believed in everything that was taught. This lasted until I was eighteen, when doubts about the Movement's goals, ideology and restrictions began to cloud a picture that had previously been clear.

I no longer wanted to be ruled by dogma and ideology. I wanted to live in my own way rather than according to rules laid down by others. I wanted self-determination at a time the Movement required obedience to the decisions of the collective group. I didn't want anybody making me feel guilty about what I did or did not do, or about what I decided regarding my own life. I did not want anyone to interfere in my personal decisions. I no longer believed in the socialism of the *kibbutz*. In short, I wanted my independence, which meant a parting of the ways. What remained was the idea to leave Chile and live in Israel. Everything else I threw out.

After I began to question the Movement, I resented the time I was required to give up for its activities. In practice, this meant that I spent more time at work, I refused to lead groups of younger members and I declined to take part in the Movement's leadership. I wanted to spend more time with Ursel, and less time with others. When there were discussions about our common future in Israel, I knew it excluded me and I no longer took any interest.

Up to the time I rejected the Movement, it had exerted a large influence on me dating from the time when I first joined in 1939. This influence was both good and bad. Its greatest contribution to my life was that it restored my sense of self-worth, which had been so severely damaged by the Nazi slogans I had absorbed and internalized. Rather than being an inferior outcast, my companions and I identified ourselves as the bright hope of the Jewish people. We wanted to create a new country and build a better society that provided a safe haven for Jews from all over the world. True, the country where we were going to establish this Utopia was occupied by others, i.e., the Arabs, but I was too young and immature to let that bother me much. To accomplish this dream, the Movement's members needed to keep themselves mentally and physically healthy. In turn that meant a moral, rather puritanical lifestyle that excluded drinking, smoking and sexual promiscuity. Drugs were not a problem at the time.

I had left school early and lacked in formal education. So did many of my comrades. To compensate, the Movement made a conscious effort to raise its member's cultural level in informal ways. I heard lectures, listened to recorded music, and was encouraged to read books, attend concerts and the theater. But often the ideology intruded even on these efforts. For example, I participated in discussions about whether a Beethoven symphony or a Titian painting were "proletarian," and artists from long ago were criticized for not being so. My reaction to this was that it was ludicrous and anachronistic, but my opinion did not carry much weight with my companions.

There is no doubt that the socialist theories I was exposed to raised my social consciousness and my sensitivity to poverty. At the same time the impact was purely theoretical. What touched my emotions and made the theories real was the opportunity I had to observe first-hand the lives of many Chilean workers who were truly poor. Without that, the teachings would have remained an intellectual exercise lacking any deeper significance.

I formed lifelong friendships with other members of my group, and in future years those friendships spanned the various countries and continents where we ended up living: Israel, Germany, Chile and the United States. When we met again years later, the former friendships returned instantly in all their intensity, so that it was as if no time had passed since we had last seen each other.

Other influences were detrimental in crucial ways. The most damaging to me over the long run was the Movement's opposition to professional studies. I believed what I was told, left school prematurely and did not pursue the engineering studies that I had dreamed about since childhood. It took me twenty years and another migration to realize my dream of becoming an engineer—something I could have accomplished in Chile in seven years instead of two decades.

The insistence on accepting the Movement's political orientation without dissent, the demand to share all my belongings with the group according to socialist doctrine and the prospect of having to submit future personal decisions to the judgment of the collective were the prime reasons for my decision to break away. I have never regretted the decision.

Girls, Love...and a Wedding

A few weeks after coming to Chile, I was invited to the house of a boy my age. I saw a girl there who I liked instantly. Her name was Ursel. I thought, "One day I will marry her." And nine years later I did. But before that could happen there were some obstacles to overcome: she had a boyfriend; I had a girlfriend and a few infatuations.

When I was twelve, I fell in love with a girl who was also a member of the *Kidma* and she became my girlfriend. Her name was Lore and she was a year younger than me. We spent a lot of time together. I was invited to her house for tea or hot chocolate, and we walked and hiked. It did not last long. One day we went for a long hike on the San Cristóbal. We walked the trails for a few hours, then came down. It was already late in the afternoon. Although Lore was not used to such long hikes, she had bravely accompanied me. Back in the city her feet hurt from the blisters she had acquired. She was crying. Incredibly, I did not take her home. I put her on a streetcar, said good-bye, and let her go home by herself. Then I went to my own house. That hike proved to be a crucial event in our relationship. After that, she was no longer my girlfriend. I felt guilty. Our puppy love was destined to fail. We were too young. Both of us never forgot the experience. In spite of it, our attachment proved strong enough that we remained friends. To this day.

I always liked Ursel, but I was not the only one who liked her. There were six boys in love with her, all at the same time. We all pursued her and demanded that she choose one of us as a boyfriend. She was twelve or thirteen at that time. I often waited for her at streetcar stops on her route home from school, and I would climb aboard the car she was in to press my case. So did my rivals. At meetings I tried to sit next to her, on hikes I tried to walk with her. She was bothered by so much attention and cried to her mother about it. Finally, to end to it all, she told the boy who climbed aboard the streetcar on that day that she had chosen him. All of us in pursuit of her were friends from the same group in the *Kidma*, and according to the dictates of our youthful code of honor, the girlfriend of our comrade was off limits for us. The boy she chose turned out to be the wrong one for her, although she remained his girlfriend for three years before they split up.

While Ursel was occupied with her boyfriend, I continued to like her and I envied him. Even so, I became passionately infatuated with another girl, who was my boss' sister and also a member of the *Kidma*. My friends were amused by the many ways I pursued her, and they made fun of me. I am sure she was not amused. In any case, my romantic stirrings went unreciprocated.

In spite of that other infatuation, I remained certain that Ursel and I were meant for each other. We often shared our thoughts and feelings. When she broke up with her boyfriend in August 1944, it was only natural that I asked myself whether she would now become my girlfriend. I thought that our affinity and instinctive understanding of each other made it inevitable. But it took time—lots of it, considering my impatience. Ursel wanted time to heal from her recent break up, and she didn't want to rush into another serious relationship. I was anxious, but did not want to ruin my chances with too much haste. On those occasions when I stayed away from her to give her the time she said she needed, my entire body was aching with a yearning to be close to her. Little by little we drifted together. It seemed almost effortless and natural. One afternoon in my house we prepared a decoration for a celebration in the Movement. We worked for a few hours and talked while we worked. Somehow, in an indefinable way, when we finished we had been irreversibly drawn together. Even so, it still took more time and I remained impatient. My diary records this fact again and again. But what occurred that afternoon would not be reversed.

Six months later I was confident that I had attained my goal: we had become boyfriend and girlfriend. A couple. Nothing was ever said, it was just there and we both understood it. In my diary entry of February 27, 1945, I quote the first line of Schiller's poem "Ode to Joy," "*Freude, schöner Götterfunken*" (Joy, radiant spark of the Gods). From this point forward, we relied on each other more and more. As early as October 1945, when I was seventeen, I wrote that I could not imagine a future without her.

Ursel was a bookbinder. She worked in a shop in a small one-room hut at the rear of the house where she lived. Her brother, who was three years older, had created the business when he was sixteen. It was a one-man business, a home industry. Ursel completed the ninth grade and then left school, just as I had done, and joined her brother in his work. After he went to the *hachsharah* and then to Israel, she ran the shop by herself. It was high-quality, artistic work, but it was also backbreaking. She picked up the books from customers and delivered them herself when hey were bound. She shopped for the leather and cloth she needed, then carried them home by herself to bind the books. At the end of her workday she was exhausted. I still have beautiful books bound in leather and printed with gold letters that she bound and then gave to me as presents—books that I love with poems by Schiller, Goethe, Heine and Pablo Neruda.

Ursel's father died in 1946 from a heart ailment he had acquired during World War I in the service of his former fatherland, Germany. He was forty-eight at the time of his death. Ursel was only eighteen, and she became an orphan. She left the house where she had been living with her father and brother and went to live with her aunt next door.

In 1947, as our doubts about the Movement began to increase, Ursel and I began to consider our common future. In 1948 we came up with the thought that it might be fun to visit the United States for a while. We also thought that it might be wise to study something that would make it easier for us to earn a living in Israel if we decided against joining a *kibbutz*, which seemed more likely with each passing day. Going to the United States would be a great adventure. We had little money and few prospects of earning more, and we saw it as perhaps our last opportunity to see a part of the world before we settled down in far-off Palestine, possibly without the means to ever leave it again. We would only stay in United States a short while, and then continue to our final destination. We would have to work while in the United States and for that an immigration visa was necessary.

Peter, my boss and now also my friend, was planning to immigrate to the United States, and it was his example that inspired Ursel and me to consider the idea for ourselves. After Peter left, he and I continued to write to each other. His glowing accounts of America further influenced our decision to follow him. He found work easily, and rented a room in an apartment of Jewish immigrants from Germany. In his letters he described the washing machine in the basement of his building, the frozen and canned food he purchased to prepare his meals and his attendance at concerts and theater performances. His descriptions were simple and superficial, but they sounded like great fun. His letters provided the push we needed to make our own decision. In this way Peter shaped the future course of our lives. He remained our friend until he died of cancer in New York many years later.

At that time, immigration visas to the United States were easy to get. They were given on the basis of the applicant's country of birth, and not the country of residence. We applied under the German quota, which was wide open because most Germans had belonged to the Nazi party and were thus ineligible for entry into the United States. That soon changed, however, and we almost lost our opportunity.

Just as in 1945 when our relationship became a fact we never explicitly expressed, Ursel and I never made an explicit commitment to marry. Instead, we understood it and considered it natural and inevitable. There was no proposal, no engagement, only the setting of the date. Neither of us popped the question, "Will you marry me?" The only question asked was, "When?" We knew that we belonged to each other, so we set the date of December 19, 1948, for a Jewish wedding to be held in the synagogue. In Chile the only legally valid marriage takes place before a justice of the peace, and this is normally performed just before the traditional religious ceremony. The paperwork was easier if we applied for the American visa as a couple, so we decided not to wait for December and got legally married on October 11. My boss and Ursel's aunt were the official witnesses, and my mother was also present. That was the entire wedding party. As far as our relatives were concerned, this was just a formality. In their view, we were not really married until after the religious ceremony had taken place. Instead of a honeymoon we had a brief afternoon tea with the other participants in a nearby restaurant, after which Ursel and I parted company and went to our own homes as if nothing had changed!

Both of us were twenty, but the legal age for marriage in Chile was twenty-one. We needed permission to marry from our closest relatives. For me that was no problem, I had my mother. But Ursel did not have any surviving parents. Her closest relative under the law was her grandmother, the mother of her mother. However, there was a problem. Everybody in Chile was required to have an identity card, both citizen and foreigner alike. Ursel's grandmother had recently been mugged on the street and her pocketbook taken. Consequently, she no longer had her identity card. Being so old, she thought she would not need it anymore and did not bother to replace it. A replacement card was expensive for a foreigner, costing about fifty times what a Chilean paid. Ursel and I went to see the judge the morning of the wedding and explained the situation. He had a suggestion: Ursel's aunt, the other daughter of the grandmother, should come in and swear that her mother was dead. Then the aunt could give Ursel permission to marry. So it was. In the afternoon, the aunt perjured herself with a straight face, swearing that her mother was dead. The judge, with an equally straight face, accepted her declaration and married us.

After we were legally married, we applied for immigration visas to the United States. We were soon notified that the visas had been granted. But we did not hurry to pick them up because we were not fully convinced that we really wanted to go.

The religious wedding in the synagogue took place as planned on December 19. A friend recorded the event on her camera outside on the street, taking two or three pictures of Ursel and me standing in front of the synagogue. That took care of the wedding photography. The ceremony was simple. There were no bridesmaids, ushers, best man or matron of honor. The father of my best friend, the man in whose high holiday choir I had sung years before and whom I had always felt close to, played the harmonium. One of the two rabbis of the congregation, the one we both liked, performed the ceremony. It turned out to be a dignified, lovely occasion. We were happy.

After the ceremony, my mother hosted a dinner in the synagogue. There were about thirty guests, all of them relatives. Mother had not invited any of our friends. We were too inexperienced, and perhaps also too intimidated by her, to ask that our closest friends be present. There were poems and songs that had been composed for the event, and toasts and speeches were made as it was an occasion to express love and good feelings. But the absence of our friends hurt.

We went to the Chilean south for our honeymoon, a paradise that has often been compared to Switzerland. We traveled by train in a luxurious private compartment. We had a marvelous time, enjoying the splendid nature and each other's company. We climbed an active volcano and crossed mountain-rimmed lakes into Argentina by boat (where trees along the forest roads were plastered with pictures of Argentina's dictator Juan Perón and his wife Evita). We ate exotic seafood found only in that region. On Christmas Eve we attended midnight mass, the *misa del gallo,* in a village church. In the pictures we took of each other, we look just like the youngsters we were! We returned from our idyllic honeymoon to face the disaster of the *hachsharah.*

Hachsharah, the Ultimate Test...and the Last Straw

In retrospect it is difficult to explain why with all our doubts we went to the *hachsharah* at all. But at the time we had not made a final break with the Movement and its ideas. It was not easy, perhaps impossible, to shake off so many years of indoctrination and also companionship with our friends all at once. We never even talked about not going. Our friends were there, we were still members of the group, and it was natural for us to go too. But we also considered it a final, definitive test of our own ideas and goals.

So in January of 1949, in spite of our doubts, we joined our fifteen or so comrades at the *hachscharah,* the farm that was meant to prepare us for life in a *kibbutz.* Four years earlier we had collected money from the Jewish community and contributed our own money to buy this farm, which had thirty dairy cows, hundreds of chickens, countless rats and a similar number mice. The farm produced corn and other grains to feed the livestock, and sold milk, butter, cream, cheese and eggs. Every few days our small pickup truck made the short trip to Santiago to sell products to members of the Jewish community. My brother was among the first to go to the farm. After his group left for Palestine as illegal immigrants, the next age group went to *hachsharah*. They left two years later, and now it was our turn.

Early one morning we left Santiago for the farm. We knew it well, it was not far. We had visited when the older members were there, and had occasionally helped them with their work. On one such occasion I had been asked to irrigate a field that was more than two acres in size. To do so, I was given a two-gallon watering can. My instructions were to fill the can from the irrigation canal next to the field, and then irrigate the field with that water, refilling the can as needed. It was a joke, but I did not know any better and did as I was told. Those who had given me this job came out to the field a little later, camera in hand, to take pictures of the city boy they had fooled. I was not amused.

We took up residence in one of the small one- and two-bedroom houses that lined the unpaved road. In our room we found two beds, two night tables, a couple of chairs and a table. Having a private room was a luxury. Due to the lack of living space, earlier married couples had had to share their rooms—sometimes with another couple, and other times with a bachelor. A curtain was all that afforded privacy. We used a neighbor's field as a toilet because we discovered upon our arrival that the farm had no functioning toilets. Many days went by before that situation was remedied. In the evening when I went to take a shower, I discovered that it did not work either.

We took our meals in the common dining room in a larger building at the end of the row of residential houses. One of our members was the cook and prepared the meals in the adjacent kitchen. Water was obtained from the single well next to the building. I attended frequent group meetings held in the dining room. We discussed the running of the farm, current problems and what to do about them. Yet nobody seemed to be in charge. Sometimes we criticized members for what they had done or not done. Ursel and I were criticized. We had not handed over our savings and we intended to stop in America before going to Israel. We did not apologize or change our plans.

The physical conditions on the farm had deteriorated and were unacceptable even for an underdeveloped country such as Chile. The non-functioning toilets and showers were but one example. The rats and mice were another. Once when we opened our night table, a mouse jumped out that had been feasting on chocolate we kept in the drawer. Ursel made butter and cheese in a tiny dark room adjacent to the cow shed. Her day started early, before six o'clock in the morning. Every morning the people who milked the cows brought a portion of the milk into the room where Ursel churned the butter in an antiquated machine that stood against one wall. Sometimes the process did not work and there was no butter at the end or the butter tasted bad and had to be discarded. To make cottage cheese, she hung a treated milk product from the rafters in sacks that dripped until the cheese was finished. Every morning she first had to knock on the door before she entered to scare the rats away. Even then, rats remained hanging from the sacks and gnawed at the cheese under preparation. The holes they made were occasionally so large that the unfinished cheese spilled to the floor. When an epidemic of typhoid broke out on the farm, it was traced to three rats that had drowned in the well that supplied our drinking water. Ripe corn kernels were spread out on the roof of the barn to dry before being stored for later use as animal feed. A large part of this crop was lost to the rats, which grew fat from feasting on the corn. The members we elected as managers to be responsible for the day-to-day operation of the farm failed to take any measures to improve the unsanitary conditions. Perhaps they did not know what to do, as they were also only twenty-year-old city boys and girls lacking farm experience.

I was assigned to work in the stables with the cows. Every day I drove the cows out to pasture, cleaned the stables, and, in the afternoon prior to milking time, I drove them back and distributed food to them. Although it was hard work, I enjoyed it. Each cow had a name and a distinctive personality. I soon got to know the characteristics and behavior of each: whether she was nervous or calm, whether she would attempt to kick me or whether she would resist being driven out of the stable. We had a bull in a separate enclosure who was violent and had to be carefully watched. In the middle of one night he was stung by bees and broke out of his enclosure. To catch him was a dangerous task, and he ran around the farm knocking against buildings and farm implements. He did a lot of damage before we were able to get him back where he belonged. The downside of my work was that I was never able to get rid of the stable smells, no matter how hard I washed myself. My work shoes were made from rubber pieces cut out of old car tires, and the tire strips were held to my feet with strings. I wore no socks. I was not used to such footwear and my feet were always sore and inflamed so that I could hardly walk. Our elected managers said they did not have the funds to buy proper footwear. They thought the tire sandals were adequate and pointed out that our Chilean farmhand wore such "shoes" and did not complain.

The farmhand, *Don* José, lived in a one-room shack that he shared with his wife, children, chickens, dog, and sometimes a pig. Onions, corn and other produce hung from the rafters. I don't know where they washed or what they used for a toilet. They did not use our facilities even when they functioned. *Don* José would steal produce out of the fields. Once I caught him stealing grapes and tried to prevent it. The farmhand threatened to beat me up. For several days after that I carried a revolver—just in case. Nobody did anything about the farmhand because he had been there from the beginning and was essential for the functioning of the farm. It was *Don* José who provided our training. During the four years he spent training these future "socialist" farmers, it had never occurred to any of them to improve his family's living conditions. Instead, they had given the family a radio as a present.

After less than two months on the farm, I left and went to live where Ursel had lived before we were married. She joined me there a few weeks later. I felt that we were finally free.

On our honeymoon, we had decided to make the American adventure come true. Even so, we had still not picked up our visas. One day the consul notified us that our visas had expired, but that as a favor he would be willing to send a telegram to Washington to request for reinstatement, provided we paid for it. We gratefully accepted the consul's offer. The visas were reinstated and this time around we wasted no time in picking them up. In good time too, because a few weeks later the German quota was opened to former members of the Nazi party who had not committed war crimes. The quota was filled almost instantly and from now on the waiting time for immigration visas required several years.

We prepared for our trip to the United States. We felt a great sense of adventure. We did not know what to expect and did not set any time limit on our stay. There were lots of possibilities. Before we left we packed a big container with everything we would need once we arrived in Israel, and then shipped the box to Israel. We never saw it again. The contents were later distributed to relatives already there.

At the same time my mother also prepared to leave Chile for Israel. She looked for a buyer of her portion of the factory. The buyer she found was the wife of the rabbi who had married us. Although she had no knowledge of this type of business, she continued to operate it together with my mother's former partner. The business folded a few years later when the rabbi and his wife moved to Israel.

Once she arrived in Israel, Mother had wanted to live in the *kibbutz* where my brother and his companions had settled. The *kibbutz* could not accept her due to its limited facilities. She settled in town instead, and at the age of sixty-three took a job as a maid. She did all the household chores for the family that employed her, and in addition, cared for their young child. The flat where she worked was three flights up, and several times a day she had to make the trip up and down the stairs as her work demanded. She had broken her leg in 1924, and it had never properly healed. As a result, she had difficulty walking. Climbing up and down the stairs made matters worse. After a while she suffered a complete physical collapse and my brother's *kibbutz* had to take her in, whether they wanted to or not. In time, the parents of other Chileans arrived. These were people Mother had known and been friendly with in Chile. Together with the other older parents she found a home in the *kibbutz* and lived there contentedly until she died in 1974 at the age of eighty-seven.

Farewell

In July 1949, we left Chile for America. We had no regrets and thought that we were leaving nothing of importance behind. We were wrong. Over the years, Chile has exerted an ever-increasing pull on us, and the sense of what we left behind made itself felt. Belatedly, we developed an appreciation of Chile and its culture, and we came to understand that the country had meant a great deal to us in spite of our almost exclusive preoccupation with Israel. More importantly, I felt a sense of gratitude. In a crucial moment of danger, Chile had opened its door and saved my life, the lives of my mother, father, and brother, and the life of the girl I would one day marry. Many years later, in the United States, I had a professional opportunity to repay the Chileans in a small measure. I helped them to develop a life-saving activity of a different kind, one that would save the lives of accident victims instead of refugees as we had been years earlier. But for now, America was waiting for us.

Interlude:
Good-bye, Chile

Puro Chile...Adiós

PASAPORTE PARA EXTRANJERO...VÁLIDO SÓLO PARA SALIR DEL PAÍS: PASSPORT for a foreigner...valid only to exit the country. These were the passports issued to us by the Chilean authorities. Our decision had become irrevocable. We were allowed to leave, but not to return. So we left behind the fields bordered with flowers, the majestic mountains and the sea that serenely bathed the country. We left behind our friends, and the Movement that we had rejected. We left behind a country that had offered us refuge in our hour of need, but had never become home. We left with some trepidation about what the future would bring, but also with a sense of adventure and the hope that in the end all would turn out well. It did, although not quite the way we imagined.

Our Chilean passports stated, falsely, that we were German citizens. We were not because a long time ago the Germans had defined a German as someone having "German blood." That continues to this day. Fifth generation descendants of German immigrants to Chile are considered Germans, as are descendants of Germans who migrated to the Ukraine many generations ago but no longer speak the language and know nothing of "their country." But Jews like me, who were born and bred in Germany, and Jews like my father who served in the German Army in World War I, Jews who shared in the German culture and contributed to its development, were not considered Germans. We, as Jews, did not have the precious German blood, and because of that, the German government had taken away our citizenship and left us stateless.

On the 13th of July 1949, Mother, Ursel and I left Santiago's Los Cerrillos airport for the short flight to Buenos Aires, Argentina. It was my first flight ever and I looked forward to the experience. A newspaper on my seat greeted me with a front-page headline that announced the crash of another plane on the same day in the same mountains we were about to cross. Fortunately, the propeller driven

Douglas DC-6 airplane, modern at that time, crossed safely. Looking out the windows I said good-bye to the mountains that had been the destination of so many of our hikes. In July, the middle of winter, they were covered with snow as far as the eye could see. It was a fitting farewell to the Andes. We would miss the mountains and it would be more than three decades before we saw them again.

During the trip, my mother carried a traditional braided Sabbath bread, a *challah*. She had baked it just before we left as an arrival offering to my cousins Martin and Curt who were waiting at the airport. Thirteen years had passed since we had last seen the two sons of Aunt Jenny, whom I had often visited in the little village of Germau. During our two week stay in Buenos Aires we lived in Martin's house. His wife, also called Ursel, had been his girlfriend in Königsberg and I was always fond of her. I was happy to see at least part of our family reunited. So few had survived.

Martin was much older than me. He confirmed the story of my father's first marriage related earlier in this account. It was the first time I heard the story, my parents had never provided any details.

Ursel and I went sightseeing in Buenos Aires. We found a modern city much like Santiago, only larger. I missed the mountains that made the Chilean capital so beautiful. On our walks I found the city uninteresting and lacking charm. When I returned decades later, that impression did not change.

Two weeks later it was time for Mother and us to separate and go our own ways. Ursel and I were to take a ship to the United States, while Mother traveled to Israel on a different ship. During our final night together, Mother, as a last farewell, scolded Ursel and me as being irresponsible adventurers for wanting to spend a few months in the United States. The outburst was unexpected and all the more surprising because she had never expressed such misgivings before. She had helped us in many ways and had even paid for the tickets for the trip. Perhaps she realized at this moment that we now were independent from her, and that henceforth we would make our decisions on our own. That must have upset her very much. The mood carried over to the next morning when we left. It was a sad parting.

Agnete

Agnete was the name of the small Danish freighter that carried cargo and a few passengers between ports along the Atlantic coasts of North and South America. Now it would carry us to the United States. There were four other passengers: an East European couple with their young daughter and an American engineer who took great pleasure in telling us again and again how bad the economic situation in the United States was and how many people were unemployed. The Agnete was a delightful home for the forty days it took to travel from Buenos Aires to New York. We were in no hurry. There was nothing that urgent awaited us in New York, and we were not sure whether we would not die of hunger once we got there. So each day on board ship was another day when we could eat and postpone the starvation we feared might follow.

We had a beautiful cabin and were attended by a friendly steward and his wife, a young couple working on the ship to earn money so that they could open a bakery in Copenhagen. We ate our meals in the captain's dining room with the captain and his three officers. It was rich Danish food, with lots of butter, many varieties of cheese, cold cuts, and meat dishes covered with fatty sauces. A special treat, unknown to us previously, was a fruit salad in mayonnaise. Every day, after an abundant breakfast, Ursel and I played three games of chess and then spent the rest of the day reading and relaxing on deck, exploring the ship and talking to crew members. A few days after we left Buenos Aires, the ship started zigzagging from left to right and right to left. The automatic steering system had broken down. As a trained radio technician I fancied that I could fix it. But I was wrong. For days I studied diagrams I did not understand, removed and replaced vacuum tubes, and adjusted controls. Nothing worked. The ship continued to zigzag and had to be manually steered until we arrived in New York.

We stopped at numerous ports in many countries, occasionally traveling up a river for days to unload cargo and take on a new load. In some places the port workers were on strike, and we had to wait for labor disputes to be settled before the ship could be loaded or unloaded. Some of these ports, particularly in the jungle forests of Brazil, were very primitive. One was Itajaí, where we loaded tapioca for the United States after waiting for the settlement of a strike. We spent days walking through this little village, curious about the primitive living conditions of the largely black population. When we were hungry, we bought bananas that were still on the branches and cut straight off the trees. The area had been settled many years ago by German colonists. As a result, some of the black children had very light, almost blond hair.

In some ports, the shipping companies hosted a dinner for the captain and his officers. Sometimes the passengers were invited along. At one such dinner in Brazil, five languages were spoken simultaneously at the table—Spanish, Portuguese, Danish, English and German. None of the participants understood more than two or three of the languages. It was like a tower of Babel, and at the end of the evening our heads were spinning, not only from the abundant wine that had been served, but even more from the linguistic confusion.

We earned some illegal spending money by selling cartons of American cigarettes in the South American ports where the ship docked. We bought the cartons at a very cheap price from the steward and carried them ashore. There was never any customs inspection and we did not have to worry about being caught. We sold them at a good profit as soon as we left the port area. Only once did things go wrong. In Bahía, one of the largest Brazilian ports, a boy approached us and offered to sell the cigarettes for us. The customer, he said, was in a large building on the side of a hill. He would sell them and then bring us the money. We gave him two cartons and waited patiently, but they boy never returned. Finally someone told us that the building had an exit on a parallel street higher up. The boy had disappeared through that exit with our cigarettes.

Close to the port of Santos is the large city of São Paulo. I was aware that a childhood friend from Königsberg lived in the city. We had been together on the Lobitten farm during our last two summer vacations in Germany. I knew his address. We took the bus to São Paulo and spent almost an entire day with him—walking, talking, sightseeing and eating. But during all those hours he could not remember me and did not know who I was. In the evening, he accompanied us to the bus that took us back to the ship. As the bus pulled out, I could see in his face that a light had gone on in a sudden remembrance. He shouted after us that now he remembered me. I never saw him again. Letters I wrote to him after we arrived in New York went unanswered. I was disappointed. Forty-eight years later I found his address by coincidence. He still lived in São Paulo and I wrote to him. This time he answered. Now, not only did he not remember me, he had also forgotten our visit in 1949. He was the first of several surviving friends that I contacted later, who, in turn, did not remember me.

We spent one night, from sundown to sunup, in Rio de Janeiro. The ship arrived in port late in the afternoon but did not dock. A little boat came broadside to take us to the city. We took the cable car up the Sugar Loaf, the huge rock which is Rio's landmark. From there we had a view of the tourist's far off Promised Land, the Copacabana beach. In the other direction we saw the Christ the Redeemer statue on top of the Corcovado mountain, which is much like the statue of the virgin on Santiago's San Cristóbal. We ambled through the streets, admiring the architecture of the many tall office buildings in the center of town. Although in later years such buildings appeared throughout the world, they were new then, having been pioneered by the Brazilian architect, Oscar Niemeyer. We admired chessboards made of butterfly wings. They only cost one dollar. We thought we could not afford that and did not buy one, an omission we have regretted ever since. Before sunrise we returned to our ship, and then slept the next day.

When we approached the United States coast we knew our trip was nearing its end, but not before we made an unscheduled stop in Jacksonville, Florida, to sit out a hurricane. It was an unexpected introduction to our new country. Loaves of sliced white bread packed in cellophane were brought on board. When I pressed just a little from both ends, I squeezed the twelve inch loaf down to one inch without any effort. I had never seen or tasted bread like that, and I did not like it. More important impressions lay in wait for us. We took the bus from the port into town, and there were signs telling black passengers to sit in the back. We were sure they were leftovers from a time long ago that somebody had forgotten to take down. After all, we had come to this great democracy where all men (and by implication, all women) were equal. At least that was what the American propaganda in Chile had taught us. We were soon disabused of such a naïve idea. In faulty English we asked a car dealer in town about it, and he laughed at our ignorance. He explained that this kind of separation was "natural." We were shocked. Otherwise he was very friendly and suggested that we settle in his town. We drank a coke in a Walgreen drugstore where, to our surprise, they not only had a lunch counter but sold everything from toys to tools. In one corner, almost out of sight, they also dispensed prescription drugs. The drugstores we had known in the past sold only what their name implied—drugs.

We left Florida after a few days, and steadily moved north. We heard American radio broadcasts, with music and newscasts that were unfamiliar to us. We understood little of what was said, but our American fellow traveler obliged us with translations, particularly when they announced the latest ever increasing unemployment figures.

The Statue of Liberty Waves "Good Morning"

We woke up early in the morning of August 31, 1949, and went on deck. The sky was blue, the sun shining and in front of us the Statue of Liberty stood waving a salute of welcome. Almost five decades have passed since our arrival, and I still remember the emotions that went through me—the exhilaration, joy, hope, and yes, the worry and fear over what the future would bring. Unlike Chile, the United States had not saved us from a terrible fate. In fact, the United States was one of those countries that had closed its doors in the time of greatest need. At that moment this strange new land did not represent a great hope for anything. We were, after all, only passing through. Yet, the moment left an indelible impression. Through the Statue of Liberty, America was extending a welcome that seemed to promise us a future of our own choosing whether we wanted it or not. The great American mystique was working overtime on my emotions.

We had brought two checks for $1,000 each. Since we lacked a sponsor who would be financially responsible for us in case of need, the checks were required for our entry into United States. It was borrowed money that we sent back to Chile as soon as we arrived. Our own money amounted to $400, which had to last until we found jobs. We also carried the obligatory chest X-rays that had been taken shortly before we applied for our visas. They were needed to prove that we did not have TB, a disease that would have barred us from entry. Little did we suspect that one of these X-rays might later be of crucial importance in assuring our continued stay.

We did not know where we would spend our first night, much less the days that followed. Nor did we know how to go about finding jobs. We spoke little English, and had no plans. New York City, with its five boroughs and eight million people, was enormous beyond imagination. We had relatives in New York, a cousin of Ursel's father and his family, and a distant relative of my father who had a daughter our age, but none of them knew we were coming. We had not bothered to tell them.

We ate our last breakfast on board the Agnete, our "Last Meal." We ate until we were stuffed because we did not know when we would get another meal. The ship docked and the American immigration agents came on board. They examined our passports, visas, X-rays and $1,000 checks, and admitted us to the United States.

When we looked over the rail at the dock, our good and faithful friend, my former boss, Peter Pfeffer, was waiting for us. We had written to him, and he had come to greet us. He was a true savior whose presence and preparations eased our worries about how we would spend our first days in the new country. We said good-bye to the friendly crew and to our fellow passengers that had shared our home for forty days, and walked down the gang plank. We had arrived!

America,
America...

ONCE AGAIN ANOTHER BEGINNING IN ANOTHER NEW LAND.
As we began our life in this country, for the first time we were truly on our own, free to shape our lives as we desired.

When we arrived we had only vague ideas about what we were going to do, how long we were going to stay, and what we would do after we left. We were too young and inexperienced to have formulated specific plans. Our idea was to study something that would help us earn a living after we got to Israel. For me, this something was related to radios. For a time I even thought about becoming a radio operator on board a commercial ship. Ursel had no plans. In the meantime we had to find work to keep us going, and then to take the appropriate steps to carry out our plans. Ultimately our lives took an unexpected turn, different from anything we had planned—a turn we never could have imagined in Chile or at that moment when we stepped on American soil.

Peter invited us to stay with him for the first few nights after our arrival. He lived in an apartment on Broadway in Manhattan. Our first surprise involved the preparation of dinner. We went to a grocery store, bought enough canned and frozen food for the meal and heated it in the kitchen. Total time spent: fifteen minutes. In Chile, the preparation of such a meal would have taken the whole day! It was the first of many surprises that awaited us over the next weeks, months and years.

We found a large and beautifully furnished room on the corner of 96th Street and Broadway. The location was similar to my first room in Chile ten years earlier: a corner room with windows looking out on one of New York's main streets, Broadway, and the other windows overlooking a principal side street. Having found a place to live, the next task was to find work.

Body and Soul

It was clear that we could not exhaust our "capital" of $400. We needed work. One of the myths we'd heard about America was that a couple could make a living by serving as a maid and butler to a wealthy family. The advantage was free room and board, so that we could save our salaries. All we had to do was to find such a setup. Ursel looked in the "New York Times" classified ads, where she found a position for a live-in nursemaid to twin eight-year-old boys a few blocks from where we were living. It was not exactly what we hoped to find, but Ursel presented herself and was offered the job. Her pay was room and board for the two of us, plus $40 a month! It sounded like the haven we were seeking. We moved out of our newly rented room and moved in with the family. We soon dis-

157

covered it was a case of crass exploitation. The couple that hired her took advantage of our inexperience, and Ursel "advanced" from being a nursemaid to cleaning the house and performing other menial tasks.

Shortly before Peter closed his store in Santiago, a customer had come in for radio repair. He was an American working for Westinghouse, and he was about to return to New York. After I repaired his radio, he and I had a pleasant, casual conversation. I told him about my plan to come to America. He gave me his business card and told me to come see him. He said that he would be glad to arrange for a job for me. In New York I went to look for him. His office was in a tall building near Wall Street. I rode the elevator up to the 25th floor, entered the Westinghouse suite, handed the receptionist the man's business card and explained to her what my visit was about. This was difficult, since I spoke little English. She dutifully took the card into the office of this apparently powerful man returning a minute later. The man had no time for me, did not recall that he had given me the card and I was not to bother him again. Disappointed, I did not yet realize that to be friendly and make empty promises was a typically American trait. Such promises meant nothing. Years later I was reminded of this incident when President Johnson invited a Pakistani camel driver to come to Washington and visit him. It was a similar sort of gesture. But the Pakistani camel driver took it seriously, saved his money and came to Washington. His arrival was an embarrassment for the president, and he did not know what to do with this poor, illiterate camel driver who was expecting to be received at the White House.

I offered my services as a radio repair technician to the many radio shops in lower Manhattan. I found occasional repair work in one store, where I repaired five or six radios in more than a week, but discovered that I'd barely earned enough for my subway fare, with only a little left over for pocket money. After a couple of weeks, I realized that I needed steady work to make a living.

I saw a newspaper ad offering television receiver production work in a factory on Long Island. I was hired and placed on an assembly line that moved a partially assembled TV set in front of me every few minutes. On each set I made twenty solder joints—adding up to a few thousand each day. The pay was ninety-eight cents an hour, and the work pace was such that I didn't even have time to blow my nose, let alone go to the bathroom. Any hesitation brought a supervisor rushing over to inquire what was wrong. In Chile I had seen Charlie Chaplin's film "Modern Times." Like everybody else, I had laughed at the droll character played by Chaplin who was working on an assembly line. I came to understand that character and the joke was no longer funny. I had never experienced anything like this. A few weeks after I started, the labor union negotiated a new contract for us. Our wages were increased by two cents to one dollar an hour. But we had to pay for that raise with an increase in the assembly line speed. I asked to be transferred to a department where they tested radios that were assembled in a different part of the factory. I was given that new job, which was a bit more interesting, but just as fast. After a few weeks, I quit. I was physically and mentally exhausted. I could not take it any longer.

Searching the newspaper ads again, I discovered that a department store called Macy's was looking for a phonograph repair technician. There were many applicants and I stood in line waiting to be interviewed. When I finally got to the front of the line, I was too late. Someone else had already been hired. But due to a heavy backlog in repair work, I was offered a temporary job. I had nothing else and I took it. Compared to what I knew and the work I had done previously, this was child's play. I worked fast and repaired dozens of the sets each day. There was none of the pressure I had experienced on the assembly line, and I enjoyed the job. My supervisor must have been impressed, because in a couple of months the permanent technician that had been hired before me was fired and I was given his job. This job offered me a fringe benefit that was as important as the money I earned. I was allowed to take my first step toward a professional career. This was made possible by a member of the family that then owned Macy's. For a while, he was my boss. He took an interest in the young immigrant, inquiring about my past history, what I wanted to do with my life, my goals and expectations. He decided to help me and urged me to begin the studies I had so far delayed. I followed his advice and he made the necessary arrangements for me to be able to combine my school work with my work in the shop. This was a golden opportunity and I made good use of it.

A Health Problem...Will We Be Deported?

Ursel was feeling a bit ill when she accepted the position as a nursemaid. During the following weeks she did not improve, and she decided to seek a doctor's advice. The doctor was an elderly immigrant shaking with Parkinson's disease. X-rays revealed a large spot on Ursel's lungs, and the doctor's diagnosis was that she had TB. This was plausible. She had suffered a slight case of it years before in Chile. There had been no antibiotics then, but she had been cured by an alternate remedy: garden rest in Santiago's perfect climate and plenty of rich food. The X-rays that had been taken six months earlier when we applied for our visas had not shown any recurrence of the disease.

This diagnosis had two immediate consequences. First, we had to tell the family with whom we were living. We had no doubt that they would fire Ursel for fear of contagion, which is precisely what they did. This was about a month after Ursel had started work, and they kicked us out of the house in an absolute panic. The other, more important consequence, was that we were now at risk of deportation. Immigrants with TB were not admitted to the United States. If Ursel was sick just two months after our arrival, she would be presumed to have entered the country with the disease, and hence subject to deportation.

We moved into a nearby rooming house where we rented a small room on the third floor. The house was run down and our room had worn furniture and threadbare carpet. A dirty window overlooked similar rooms a few feet away from ours across a narrow light shaft. The building did not have an elevator, and we shared the third floor bathroom and kitchen with tenants from four other rooms. One day in the kitchen, Ursel and I, speaking in Spanish, complained bitterly about the sloppy habits of a German woman who was our neighbor. She replied in Spanish, and had obviously understood everything we had said. She told us that we did not have to go to the trouble of conversing in Spanish, and that she had no intention of changing. One night another neighbor knocked on our door. She claimed an emergency and asked to borrow some money. She promised she would return it in a few days. I gave her all we had—seven dollars. Not only did she fail to return the money, she was offended and furious when I dared ask for it.

We needed help: to cure the disease and to avoid deportation. We contacted a Jewish immigrant aid society and presented our case to them: the diagnosis of TB and our concern about being deported as a consequence. The society agreed to provide help in the form of arranging Ursel's admission to a special hospital. But without money, and a knowledge of how to "work the system," such arrangements took time. While we waited for admission to the hospital, Ursel stayed in bed. The doctor's recommendation was to "bathe her lungs in fat." So I fed her, and fed her, and fed her—lots of eggs, butter, and cheese. Within a few weeks not only her lungs were bathed in fat. She had gained more than twenty pounds!

After six weeks, we finally were given an appointment at a hospital for an initial evaluation. New X-rays were taken, laboratory tests were performed and Ursel was thoroughly examined. Then we were sent home to wait for the results. After more waiting we were told that she did not have TB. She had simply been suffering the aftereffects of the flu. The spot on the X-rays was a shadow from the pendant Ursel was wearing during the first examination. The doctor had failed to notice the necklace before he took the X-rays. Thus, the threat to her health and our fear of deportation were eliminated.

Once again, Ursel began looking for work. The maid-and-butler myth no longer had any appeal for us. She found a series of bookbinder jobs, none of which was satisfactory. Even though she was an expert who knew every step of the bookbinding process, the work was done assembly line fashion. All day long Ursel repetitively performed just a few of the steps. It was mind-numbing work similar to what I had experienced on the television assembly line. Finally she found a position at the bookbindery in the Columbia University library. There was no assembly line, and she was able to use her knowledge and skill. She liked the work, and she liked the environment and her co-workers. Ursel also took full advantage of an important fringe benefit which let her enroll in courses taught at the university. She stayed at Columbia until our first child, Ruth, was born in 1953.

Our New Family

Soon after our arrival, we got in touch with the two families in New York that were our relatives. We visited "*Tante* Erna" (Birkenfeld) and her daughter Ilse who was our age. They were distantly related to my father and I remembered them from Königsberg. We never developed a close relationship.

It was different with Ursel's relatives. Stephan Jakubowski was a cousin of Ursel's father. He, his wife, Ellie, and their daughter, Lore, instantly became our real family. They lived just a few blocks from us and this made it easy to visit. Stephan helped me to prepare my first federal income tax return. Our combined income for 1950 was about $5,000. I complained that on even that small amount we had to pay $550 in taxes. Stephan's reply was that I should be happy that I had any income on which to pay taxes at all. I still don't like taxes but even so, it was a lesson I never forgot. Stephan sent us to his doctor when we needed one. The doctor turned out to have known Ursel's father as a colleague in Berlin and this provided us with a personal doctor-patient relationship. In Stephan and Ellie we had a new set of parents. We went to their home for Sabbath evening meals, on weekends, and any time we needed them or wanted their company. We always felt welcome in their apartment. They had an empty room in the apartment and at one point talked about inviting us to move in with them. To our great sorrow, this family relationship was destined not to last. Ellie, aged fifty-four, died of cancer in June 1950, a mere nine months after we first set foot in their apartment. After she was gone, Stephan was sad and withdrawn. They had been married for thirty years and he never overcame the loss of his wife. Our visits cheered him up, but the effect did not last long. A little more than a year later he had a heart attack and died. I am sure that grief ended his life. We now mourned both of them and when our first son was born we named him Steven, in memory of "*Onkel Stephan.*"

Lore was six years older than us. She was an active young woman with a large circle of friends. We attended her wedding, the date of which was advanced from that originally planned so that Ellie was still alive to see her daughter get married. It was a happy, yet sad, occasion. Ellie's impending death was on all of our minds. Eric, Lore's new husband, was a watchmaker. The two were a perfect match, completely happy with each other. After their wedding, they lived in the Jakubowski's family apartment. We liked Eric and formed a foursome of friends. Eric was tall, good looking and very intellectual. He could discuss philosophy, history, and many other subjects that I had never thought much about. Although he was more than fifteen years older than us, the four of us behaved like children. On one occasion we drove to a park not far from the city, where we rented a boat to row out on the lake. The day was hot. Eric and I wanted to cool off, so we stripped off our pants and jumped naked into the lake. It was not the expected thing to do. The girls just laughed. There were few other boats on the lake, and I do not remember if anyone in those boats objected.

One day, when Eric was using a special machine in his shop to clean watches, it exploded and he was badly burned. Fortunately, his injuries were not life threatening. After a lengthy hospitalization, he was ready to come home on *Hanukkah* Eve, December 1951. The night before Eric's release Lore came to celebrate the festival with us. As a present, we gave her a recording of a string quartet by Schubert called "Death and the Maiden." Lore came home that evening and received a phone call informing her that Eric had died of a blood clot! Since then many years have passed, but even now Ursel and I cannot listen to "Death and the Maiden" without shivers running down our spines. Two months after Stephan's death, we went back again to Riverside Chapel in New York for a funeral—the third Jakubowski family funeral in eighteen months. In that time Lore had lost her mother, her father and her husband. We grieved with her, but could do little else to help her bear this burden.

I owe my "American" name to Lore. The very first time we met she announced that it would not do to be called Siegfried four years after the end of World War II. She named me Fred. The name stuck. When I became a US citizen in 1954, it became official and Siegfried became my middle name. Ursel came to be called Sue.

Surprises!

Life in New York was full of surprises and unexpected impressions.

I was surprised by the ease with which we were able to prepare our meals. In Chile, food preparation took hours. We'd go shopping and then cleaned the vegetables, chicken or fish and cooked everything from scratch. Often the maids did the work. Even people with little money could afford maids because the pay was so low. In New York, we went downstairs to a grocery, bought frozen or canned food—from soups to deserts and everything in between—and our meal was ready in less than half an hour.

I was surprised by the throwaway society we encountered. So many things were discarded that in Chile would have been repaired—clothing, cars, radios and appliances all got tossed. In Santiago, there were women sitting in the entrances of business buildings taking up runs in stockings. Ursel's search for such women in New York was a standing joke with us. The mother of the boys for whom Ursel cared for on her first job gave me two broken radios, and asked me to repair the better one and to throw away the other one. In Chile, a radio was never thrown away, whatever its age. I had repaired radios from the early 1920s that dated back to the dawn of radio technology. Lore's husband, Eric, offered to sell me his old but serviceable 1940 model car for fifty dollars. I did not want it, and he simply abandoned it on the street. Four years earlier in Santiago, Peter Pfeffer had driven a 1928 Ford and was proud of it.

I was surprised by the Jewish presence in New York. On average, every third or fourth person I met was Jewish. There were between two and three million Jews in the city. They worked at all kinds of trades and occupations. I met Jews who were factory workers, stock boys at Macy's and policemen. I also met craftsmen, doctors, lawyers, merchants and politicians. In all of Chile there were perhaps 30,000 or even 40,000 Jews, and most of them middle or upper class.

I was surprised by the concrete canyons of Wall Street. Prior to coming to New York, I had never seen buildings taller than ten or twelve stories. I was awed by huge skyscrapers that lined the narrow streets of the financial district, where the sky was all but invisible.

I was surprised by the advertisements on the buildings of Times Square. Their bright lights converted night into day: billboards with moving images that constantly changed colors, a huge face that blew smoke into the air from a lit cigarette and a running newscast with moving bright letters running round and round the "New York Times" building.

I was surprised by the many friends and co-workers we met who were in psychiatric care. Freudian therapy seemed a precondition to the good life. It was chic, the mark of sophistication. In my naïveté, all of these individuals seemed perfectly healthy. I had not known a single psychiatrist in Chile, where none of our friends were in such care.

I was surprised and impressed by a convincing proof of freedom. At a table set up on Broadway, I signed a petition requesting that Julius and Ethel Rosenberg, who had been convicted of atomic espionage, be spared from execution. That would have been unthinkable in Chile, let alone Nazi Germany. That expression of freedom was almost enough to want to make me stay in the United States. Chile was nominally democratic at that time, but there were tight limits on the freedoms people were allowed to enjoy. I had witnessed a peaceful, political demonstration in the center of Santiago that was fired upon by military troops. A half dozen demonstrators were killed. I witnessed the survivors marching through the streets waving the bloody shirts of the dead. Chile's "democratic" history was full of such incidents, many of them even more violent.

I was surprised that so few people asked us where we had come from. With so many in the population themselves of foreign origin, we did not stand out.

Finally, I was surprised that I felt "at home" so quickly. Just a few months after our arrival, I felt like I belonged—a feeling I had never experienced in Chile or Germany.

Settling in

We lived in the run down rooming house for a little more than a year, and then moved into an apartment of Jewish immigrants from Germany by the name of Ball. They were of our parents' generation. Their three grown sons had moved out, and their rooms were empty. To us, it seemed as if the parents sought a replacement for their children through us. We did not mind.

In 1951, I enrolled in a Technical Institute run by the RCA Company to study electrical engineering. It was a twenty-seven-month course without any breaks. The RCA Institute could not grant a regular Bachelor's degree to its graduates because it taught only engineering courses and no humanities. However, the technical curriculum was on a university level, if not higher. I chose the institute because the move to Israel was still on our minds. The sooner I finished, the sooner we could leave.

I needed a quiet room to study and do my homework. The Balls offered us a perfect arrangement. We now had two rooms, a large one where we lived and slept and a small one where I studied and did my homework. A sink off our main room and a small bathroom in the back the study filled our needs. We shared the main bath and the kitchen with the family.

The Balls were friendly people. In the more than two years we spent with them we never had any problems, in spite of the shared facilities and the fact that in January 1953, we brought our newborn daughter into the apartment. Inevitably, Ruth's birth changed everyone's normal routine. But the Balls simply accepted Ruth as a granddaughter, and welcomed our new family member to the household. On the night she was born, when Ursel felt contractions in the middle of the night, we woke a nephew of the Ball's who also lived in the apartment. He had a car and had promised to take us to the hospital. It was a maternity hospital, and when we arrived at three in the morning, a sleepy guard opened the door. The three of us walked in: highly pregnant Ursel, the nephew and I. The guard's first question was, "Who is the patient?" I was not allowed to stay with Ursel and was sent home. The next morning I had an important test at school. The professor saw me fidgeting. I was not concentrating and was not writing. He came over and asked me what the problem was. I told him that at that very moment my wife was in the hospital giving birth. He instantly dismissed me and I was given a passing grade on the test, even though I never took it. By the time I got to the hospital, Ruth had been born. I went up to see Ursel and found her still groggy from the anesthesia. Upon seeing me, she asked, "When is the baby going to be born?" She was unaware that we had a beautiful daughter, who had been born on the 27th of January; a birthday gift to her twenty-five-year-old mother.

Fritz Ball had been a lawyer in Germany. He was also a superb cellist and a good pianist. After Crystal Night, he was sent to a concentration camp where his right hand, the one he used to bow, had been crippled by frost. Even so, he continued to play both the cello and the piano. Like all German lawyers, he could not practice his profession in the United States. He worked as a simple clerk in the philanthropic CARE organization. To him it was a demeaning loss of professional standing to which he never adjusted. His music became the most important activity in his life, and twice a week he played chamber music in the apartment with other immigrant musicians. We always listened, not just to the music, but to the players' arguments about interpretation, technique, tempi and dynamics. The apartment became our music school and Fritz Ball our mentor. To his musical evenings we owe our love and understanding of chamber music and the pleasure it continues to provide us.

We had found a home and settled in. We worked; we studied; we had relatives and friends; we had many reasons to be content. Even so, we were still preparing for departure to Israel. We bought a sewing machine and radio repair instruments designed to operate on the electric power used in Israel but not in the United States. I searched for jobs in Israel and even had interviews in New York, but never received an offer. As the days, months and years drifted one into the other, it gradually dawned on us that we were in America to stay. We never made a final decision. We just kept postponing our departure. Once Ursel became pregnant and Ruth was born, the decision became manifest: there would be no further migration.

While we were procrastinating the long-planned departure, many of our friends and former comrades from the Movement left Chile for Israel and settled into the communal life of the *kibbutz*. They sensed that we would never join them, and a few wrote us letters that denounced us as traitors. Some of these letters were from the same people who had been close friends. We were hurt, but they no longer had the power to influence our decisions.

War, Again

In June 1950, less than a year after we came to America, I saw headlines in the newspapers proclaiming an American "police action" had started in far away Korea. I did not know where Korea was, and the term "police action" was a political euphemism invented by President Truman to commit the country to a war without congressional approval. The draft loomed over me. Although I was not a citizen, and had not even been able to fully master the language, I was subject to the draft law and received a letter "inviting" me to present myself for a physical. I passed and was classified 1A, the most eligible category for a call up. But I was not about to fight and die in a far-off country, the name of which I had never even heard and for a cause that I did not understand. To avoid such a fate, we needed to be prepared to leave the United States at a moment's notice. But how? We were stateless immigrants. Our Chilean passports were no longer valid and, in any case, they did not allow us to return.

By this time Germany had passed a law allowing former citizens made stateless by Nazi racial laws to reacquire their German citizenship. We applied at the German consulate in New York, and in a very short time we were Germans once again. This made us eligible to acquire valid German passports. Although we had made no plans for where we would go if we had to leave, Israel would have been the logical choice. But we would have been willing to consider other options.

Leaving the United States was one possible solution to the draft. The other was to obtain a deferment. Initially, married men where exempt. I was married and therefore in no immediate danger. As the casualties in Korea mounted and more soldiers were needed to replace the casualties, married men lost their special status and were being inducted. Certain categories of students remained exempt, engineering among them. Because I was an engineering student at the RCA Institute, I was exempt as long as I stayed in school. But as the war continued, the exemptions were gradually phased out and students were also being drafted. Fortunately, fathers were given exemptions—a father being defined as one who had children living in his household or whose wife was pregnant. When Ursel became pregnant, the certificate from her doctor gave me my final deferment.

Catching Up with Our Education

We both started studying to catch up with the education we had missed out on in Chile. Ursel took courses in music, literature and science at Columbia University. She did so just "for fun," but in the process took all of her required examinations and passed with flying colors. She was not thinking of a professional career, but years later when she did, all of her Columbia courses were accepted by her university, which significantly shortened her years of study.

To study at a technical institute, such as the RCA Institutes, instead of obtaining a regular university degree was no disadvantage in my search for employment. When I graduated with honors, I applied for a prestigious research position at the RCA Laboratories. I competed against graduates from some of the best engineering schools in New York, including Columbia University and the Brooklyn Polytechnic Institute. I was delighted when I was selected over the other applicants.

Earning a (Serious) Living...

Ursel quit her job at Columbia University in January 1953, a few weeks before Ruth was born. Because we had finally abandoned the idea of living in Israel, it was now time for me to find professional work and earn a living for our family. I started to look several months before I graduated in May of that year, but I faced two disadvantages. One was that I was not a citizen. The Korean war was still in progress and most of the positions available were for military work that required a security clearance that I, a non-citizen, could not obtain. The other reason was unexpected: I was Jewish.

Early in 1953, I saw an ad for an engineering position at IBM. I applied and the company invited me to come to the town of Endicott in upstate New York for an interview. They sent me a train ticket, and when I arrived, an IBM car was waiting to pick me up. I spoke with several people and was interested in a couple of different positions. Glancing at the forms two of the interviewers had filled out, I saw they thought I would be ideally suited for a position in their respective departments. Lunch time came around and I was taken to the executive dining room. The plan was that in the afternoon there would be one last interview with a high level executive, after which I would discuss future employment with the personnel department. During lunch, I casually asked if there was a Jewish community center or a synagogue in Endicott. The smiles froze and lunch was hurriedly completed. They brought up a car, took me back to the train station and that was the last I heard from them. I could not understand what had happened. One moment I was being actively courted, and then I was suddenly dismissed. Of course, I did not know that IBM did not hire Jews. I was still very naïve about American society and the importance attached to ethnic backgrounds. Four years earlier we did not believe it when we saw that black passengers had to sit in the back of the Florida buses, and now we found we were victimized by similar attitudes regarding Jews.

When I graduated, I accepted the research position at RCA Laboratories for which I had competed. I had been overjoyed by the offer, and I thought of it as a dream job. But to my disappointment, I soon found that the job was not what I had expected. It involved empirical experimentation on circuits for color television receivers. My mind was more analytical, and empirical experimentation was not my strongest asset. The situation reminded me of my first job in Chile, where I had lasted just five weeks. On this job I lasted five months, although I realized during my first hour at work that I had made a mistake in accepting the job.

I remained for the five months only because I could not get the security clearance that was required for most positions. Even if I applied for commercial work, a security clearance was a must if the commercial work was located in the same building where classified work was also being done. I responded to dozens of newspaper ads and sent out scores of applications. The answer that came back was always the same: no citizenship, no job.

Eventually, I got an offer from the Stromberg-Carlson Company in Rochester, New York. They produced defense and commercial electronic systems, but in separate buildings, so that the lack of a security clearance was no problem. I accepted, which meant leaving New York City and all that it offered: family and friends, museums, music and theater. A new adjustment was required, this time to a mid-sized American town, which seemed like a real small town to me. We did not know what to expect.

Before I received confirmation of the promised position, a behind-the-scenes drama played itself out in Rochester. Once again, the problem was that I was Jewish. A key engineer at Stromberg-Carlson had interviewed me in New York. He had offered jobs to two other engineers in addition to me. By coincidence all three of us were Jewish. When he returned to Rochester, his boss, a department head, looked at the applications and told the engineer to throw them in the wastebasket. The company's policy was not to hire Jews. In fact, they had never done so and he refused to be the first to break the rule. In reply, the engineer told him that if he failed to hire us, he would quit. That courageous stand carried the day, and we were hired. I found out what had happened only after I started work. I was impressed by this man's courage and have never forgotten it. The three of us were the first Jews to break the company's racial hiring barrier—or, at least that's what Stromberg-Carlson thought. In fact, they did have one Jew on their staff but they did not know it. He was a red-haired Canadian engineer. They had not asked him about his religion and he had no reason to mention it. He was an ardent Zionist, a member of the same *Hashomer Hatzaïr* Movement we had belonged to in Chile. He later made good on his beliefs, left Stromberg-Carlson and moved with his family to Israel.

In November 1953, we said good-bye to New York, to the Balls, to cousin Lore, to Peter and our other friends and to the exciting city that had been our first home in America. We came to a beautiful town, but one that was cold, cloudy and snowy for much of the year. The parks were full of beautiful flowers during the short summer, and there was a beach on the lake that we liked to visit on weekends. In Rochester we found few of the cultural amenities we took for granted in New York, and we missed them terribly. We listened to concerts performed by a mediocre symphony orchestra most of whose members were still students at the local music school; the art in the museum hardly deserved that name; theater performances were given by an amateur group and we never found any restaurants where we enjoyed the food.

In late November, I had moved to Rochester ahead of the family to find living accommodations. Every morning when I awoke in my rented room, I looked out the window and saw a dark, gray sky, the same dark sky for a whole month. I'd walk to work through depressing drizzles or snow flurries. I didn't know anyone and my only conversation during the day was with my fellow employees on the job. I felt so lonely and depressed that I wanted to turn around and go back to New York City.

I found a tiny apartment in an old two-family frame house, a mile away from my place of work. It had two small bedrooms and a small living room. A door in the back of the kitchen gave access to a tiny bathroom. I bought some furniture and some cooking utensils and made the apartment ready to live in. This cozy apartment was the first apartment where we were able to live on our own since our wedding five years earlier. Ursel and Ruth joined me on Christmas Eve, which I thought of as a wonderful Christmas present. From that day forward everything was better. Even the oppressive gray sky did not bother me as much.

Most days I walked to work. Due to the severe weather, few people ventured outside in winter so we did not meet any of our neighbors until spring. When summer arrived, we learned how to drive and bought our first car, a six-year-old Dodge. We acquired a few friends but our social life remained rather quiet.

Two memorable events occurred in Rochester. Our first son, Steven, was born in September 1954, and we became American citizens later that same year. When Ursel gave birth, I was not allowed to be in the room with her. I went home in mid-afternoon to take care of Ruth and waited for the phone to ring. When the call finally came in the early evening, I left Ruth in the care of my mother (who had arrived on a visit from Israel a few days earlier) and rushed to the hospital to see Ursel and meet my new son. All was well, and a few days later they came home.

To receive American citizenship was a proud event. Born in Germany, we had been deprived of our rights of citizenship. We had gone to Chile not by choice, but because it offered us the only refuge available. The Chilean government also withheld citizenship from us. We had come to America on our own free will, and although initially we had not wanted to stay, we had come to appreciate the country enough to want to make it our permanent home. Citizenship reconfirmed that choice and made it official.

Although there was not much for us to do in Rochester, our two little children kept us busy. My mother had come to stay for a year. She arrived in New York by ship ten days before Steven's birth, and I traveled by plane to pick her up. American Airlines offered a special rate for tickets bought for "Mr. and Mrs." My mother was Mrs. Flatow, I was Mr. Flatow, so I bought a discounted ticket for the return flight. When we came to check in at the airport, the attendants gave us strange looks, but they honored the tickets. Mother was sixty-eight years old, I was twenty-six.

In our little apartment, we had no room for Mother so we rented a furnished room for her across the street. Mother knew no English, and lacking any other friends, she required a lot of attention from us. We had a nice old lady as a neighbor who occasionally came over to help us, particularly right after we brought the new baby home. She came to our house to meet Mother and converse with her. Although they had no common language, they told each other long stories out of their lives. Ursel sat at the table and translated. Household chores went undone, but the stories needed to be finished. In the end we were lucky. Seemingly out of nowhere, a woman suddenly appeared who had shared a room with my mother in Königsberg forty years earlier and was now living in Rochester just a few blocks from us. I don't remember how this happened. In any case, the two women started to spend much time together and we got some relief.

On days when we went to the beach in the summer, our car was loaded as if it was a moving van. A playpen, a chair for mother, toys, bottles and coolers with drinks and food—as much as the car could hold. On other days we went to Niagara Falls, which was a ride of about sixty miles. The falls presented a different appearance and feel for each season, and they were particularly impressive during the cold winter months. The frozen spray on rocks and trees, the ice and snow, made them look like a brilliant fantasy land, especially on those rare winter days when the sun was shining.

We did not like living in Rochester. The severe weather, the small town atmosphere, the lack of close friends and the scarcity of cultural amenities contributed to a feeling of discontent. Twenty months after our arrival, the opportunity arose to leave the city and we left without any regrets—albeit for an uncertain future.

What we thought of as an uncertain future soon became an adventurous one. For the next seven years I worked for the Navy, sharing lives, food and sleeping arrangements with sailors and officers as I accompanied them on maneuvers. Aboard Naval aircraft, I flew to many cities in Europe, to North Africa and over the Mediterranean Sea. We lived on an exotic island in the Mediterranean the like of which we had never seen before, and we visited Israel for the first time. We also explored a number of European countries.

The way this adventure came about was that Stromberg-Carlson received a contract from the US Navy to provide field engineers for Naval support wherever they were needed. When I had joined the company, I had worked as a television receiver engineer and my responsibility had been to resolve technical problems in newly designed receivers. After I became a citizen and received my security clearance, I did similar work on electronic navigation equipment for Naval aircraft. It was interesting work that suited me well. In the fall of 1955, the company offered me one of the new field engineering positions and I accepted. I was to become a specialist in airborne anti-submarine warfare (ASW).

We sold our furniture, left our cozy apartment in Rochester, stored a few objects in the attic of a neighbor's house and initiated a gypsy life, during which we moved five times in five years. Ruth was two-and-half-years-old, Steven was one-year-old. We started the trip in our seven-year-old car, which was not in very good condition. We loaded it with our personal belongings, which were stored in the trunk of the car and on the roof in an open carrier protected from the rain by a canvass tarpaulin, as well as in every available little space inside not taken up by us or the children. One of the things we kept handy was a potty chair. Ruth was being toilet trained and every once in a while we stopped at the side of the road, dragged the potty chair out of the car and placed her on top of it. We carried a small metal cabinet filled with the children's toys. It survived on the roof under the canvass. Our first destination was Washington, DC, where I underwent training in my new field. After six weeks of that I was assigned to the Marine air base at Opa-Locka in Florida, just north of Miami.

We loaded the car as we had done in Rochester and set off on a trip which, without superhighways, lasted several days. Along the route the engine of the car sputtered and occasionally backfired with a loud *bang*. At a gas station in Virginia a mechanic said it was nothing, that all we needed was a little adjustment of the carburetor, and he sent us on our way. The engine continued to sputter and the backfiring grew increasingly worse. In Wilmington, North Carolina, the car threatened to die. Mostly, it backfired and hardly moved. We stopped at a repair shop where we were told the engine needed a major overhaul. It was an early morning at the end of December and the weather was bitter cold. The car was to be ready by evening. It did not occur to us to rent a hotel room for the day because we had so little money. We had to live hand-to-mouth on what I earned. With our little children in tow we walked the town for the next ten hours. We stopped at the train station seeking warmth, but the station was cold. We went to a department store and hid from the cold for the remaining hours. Finally the car was repaired and we set off again. When we got to Miami on New Year's Eve, we rented a furnished house from a real estate agent sight unseen. When we entered, we found a filthy mess. Every piece of furniture smelled of urine, and it was cold. We spent the evening cleaning the house and trying to keep the children warm by turning on the burners of the electric stove. There was no other heat. We lived in that filth for another month until the agent got us a new house. When I went to take possession of it a man armed with a shotgun came out and said he would shoot me if I advanced another step. I did not. Nobody intervened, not the agent, nor the police. They claimed that there was nothing they could do.

After another few weeks we were finally able to move into a better house. It was located at the end of the runway of the Marine air base, and every time a plane took off it flew low over our house and shook the furniture. Steven would scream with fear. This seemed an inauspicious beginning. The only saving grace was the beach, which we visited frequently once the weather was warm enough.

At the supermarket I found separate water fountains and rest rooms for blacks and whites. A friend fleeing from the snow in Rochester came to stay with us, and she brought her one-year-old baby. When I went out to rent a crib, the store owner made me sign a piece of paper stating that the crib would only be used by a white child and that no black child would sleep in it.

We stayed for six months, then drove back to Washington, and after another six weeks set off to my new assignment in the Mediterranean. I was detailed to a Navy base on the island of Malta. I had volunteered for the assignment because it was close to Israel, where family and friends lived. We thought it would be easier and cheaper to visit from Malta than from the United States, and we remained in Malta for the next three years until 1959.

A Maltese Interlude

Our stay on Malta was the great adventure of our lives. It was so unusual, so different from anything else in our past, that I want to linger a bit in telling about it.

How to describe this poor, primitive, picturesque island? Malta[1] was then ruled as a crown colony by the British for their own benefit and profit. The island is located about forty miles south of Sicily. It is seventeen miles long and about half as wide. The language, Maltese, is not spoken anywhere else in the world. It is close to Arabic, but there are theories claiming the origin to be the old Phoenician language. There are no lakes, no rivers, no natural resources and very few trees. In the past there were more trees but they were cut down and used for fuel during a lengthy German siege during World War II.

At that time, the island had about 300,000 inhabitants, far too many. The barren soil could not produce enough food for its ever growing population. There was so little water that it had to be imported on tanker ships in the hot summer season. The dominant Catholic Church was almost medieval in its outlook and

---

[1] The description of Malta in the following paragraphs pertains to the time we were there. Malta attained its independence in 1964. Since then it has become industrialized and a tourist haven soliciting customers throughout the world. There are many new hotels, including a Hilton and Holiday Inn, conference centers, casinos and in secluded corners of some beaches there is nude and topless bathing. The Church has lost much of its former influence.

strictly enforced its rules. It was so backward that Catholic American Navy personnel did not feel bound by the Archbishop's dictates. Instead, they followed the rules of their American prelates back home. There was no divorce and no means for birth control were sold in any of the island's pharmacies. The Maltese claimed that if a couple did not produce a baby within a year of their marriage, the parish priest would come around to see if he could help! As a result, many families, especially the poor, had countless children. In the past many of them had died, but with a sharp decrease in infant mortality, the island faced a constantly increasing population, which meant the local economy was less and less able to feed and provide work for its people. The local population became a product for export! The Maltese government actively encouraged emigration, mostly to Canada and Australia, and would pay for passage of emigrants and provide financial subsidies to them. In spite of the poverty, violent crime was almost unknown on the island. There had been a murder one year before our arrival, and people were still talking about it. There wasn't a single additional murder on the island during the three years we lived there.

Malta had a very long history from prehistoric to modern times. Beginning with the ancient Phoenicians to the current British rulers, the island had been occupied by Greeks, Romans, Arabs, Normans, Spaniards and the French. All of these occupiers left their marks and imprints.

We bought a used Volkswagen and roamed all over the island in it. As in Britain, cars were driven on the left side of the road. It was difficult to get used to that. Shortly after we arrived, I was driving happily on the right side when another car was coming straight at me. My first reaction was to curse the Maltese, exclaiming that they didn't know how to drive. At the very last moment I realized that it was I who did not know the local traffic laws, and I veered into the left lane. It was a close escape! I never made that mistake again. The narrow roads were often clogged with sheep and goat herds. As we drove, we frequently had to suddenly stop and wait until the shepherd moved his herd out of the way. The ruins of 5,000-year-old prehistoric temples, old Roman remains, catacombs, a grotto reached by a little boat, and bays and beaches offered endless wonder and fascination, and competed for our attention. Often we drove along the coast to eat freshly caught fish in one of the numerous little restaurants that dotted the road.

Valetta, the capital, is a walled city founded in 1571. Its main entrance is through a medieval gate, barely wide enough for cars. The city was so small that I could walk from this gate at one end to the sea at the other in ten minutes, a distance of ten or twelve blocks. Similar gates guarded the entrances of other small towns.

Several parallel streets led to the sea. The main street was Kings Way, and it was crowded with small family-owned shops. These shops had a three-tiered price structure. Maltese paid the least. The next higher prices were paid by British customers. Americans paid the most, all for the same merchandise. Some of my American colleagues developed a defensive strategy. They sent a British or Maltese friend to do the shopping for them. Sometimes we went to the movie house on Kings Way. The Archbishop of Malta banned an American movie, the musical "Pal Joey", as obscene and did not allow any Catholic to see it. When Ursel and I were in the town, we had iced coffee and small canapé sandwiches at the little Café Cordina. From its outside tables we had a spectacular view of the magnificent St. John's Cathedral, which had been built in 1577. Like many of the island's churches, the cathedral had two clocks, one indicating the real time, the other a false one. The false clock permanently indicated the same time to confuse the devil.

Some of the other streets leading to the sea had steps instead of a roadway. Old three- and four-story yellow sandstone houses faced each other across the narrow street. Laundry was hung out to dry, and it often spanned the street from one side to the other. Most of the children in these streets were poorly dressed and not very clean. Yet they did not look hungry and they did not beg. Many of the older women and some of the younger ones went about dressed in *faldettas*, a typical Maltese black garment covering the body from head to toe.

Before the Second World War, little Malta had a magnificent opera house in Valetta. Unfortunately, the opera house was destroyed, along with 20,000 other houses on the island, during the heavy bombing Malta suffered for two years from 1940 to 1942. The site was still full of rubble, a depressing sight. Opera was now performed in a movie house in another little town. We wanted to introduce Ruth, aged five, to opera, and we took her to a performance of Verdi's "Aida." It was in the evening and she was tired. All she remembered afterwards was that we bought her candy during each intermission.

We went for long walks along the harbor, surrounded by fortresses, walls and watch towers built by the Order of Maltese Knights that ruled the island from the sixteenth to the eighteenth century, when they were forced to surrender the island to Napoleon. Colorful little boats, *dghajsas* (pronounced "daisa"), similar to Venetian gondolas, offered transport and pleasure rides in Valetta's harbor and the bays around the island.

Ursel and I sometimes ate dinner in the best restaurant on the island, located just outside the Valetta gate in the elegant, British-owned Hotel Phoenicia. The cost of an excellent meal was only one Maltese pound, which was less than three dollars at the prevailing exchange rate! The waiters were dressed in white with gold trim, and once Ursel mistook a British admiral, who was also dressed in white with gold trim, for a waiter and asked him to get us a table. She realized her mistake only after he answered, in a very dignified way, "Madam, you must ask a waiter."

During the long summers we drove to beaches hidden away in little coves. At other times we went to the British officer's beach, which we were permitted to use because of my officer status in the Navy. For just a few pennies we could rent chairs and umbrellas, and waiters served us drinks and little sandwiches. The poorer Maltese used a beach at the foot of Valetta. The Church considered bathing suits immoral and forbade women to wear them. Instead, the women swam and sun-bathed in their underwear, which, when wet revealed more than any bathing suit ever could.

The British had installed an electric power system on the island that had been used early in the century in Britain before it was discarded. The system provided 240 volts at a frequency not used anywhere else in the world. This prevented the use of most electric appliances. Our refrigerators ran on kerosene or bottled gas, and we could not use our phonograph. There were no Maltese radio stations, but we could listen to the BBC broadcasts piped into households by wires, much like telephone lines with loudspeakers connected. It was like cable TV except is was for radio and it offered only one channel. We had no telephone. Such service was practically non-existent for private residences.

It took me thirty minutes every morning to drive to Halfar, the Navy base at the other end of the island that the United States shared with the British. On the way I passed through villages with streets so narrow that only one car could pass, although they were designated as two-way streets. Once on a sightseeing trip to the ancient fortified city of Mdina, we even got stuck with our Volkswagen in one of these streets, it was so narrow.

Each little village had a church dedicated to its particular saint. On that saint's day, the village celebrated with fireworks. Villages competed with one another as to which provided the grandest fireworks display of the year. Most often it was Lija, a village in walking distance from where we lived. In the evening of its saint's day, we stood on the roof of our house and watched the most elaborate, spectacular fireworks we have ever seen.

The furnished apartment we rented was on the first floor of a three story house in Balzan, where most of the Americans lived. The apartment was quite spacious but very simple. We had a kerosene refrigerator, and a stove and water heater that ran on bottled gas. We had no way to tell how much gas was left in the cylinder. Our kitchen had a dual setup, the water heater in the bathroom did not. Often it ran out of gas as I was taking a shower. Portable kerosene space heaters provided scant relief during the chilly winters. The building code required that each room had to be vented by an opening high up in the wall, about ten-by-six-inches in size. Cold winds blew through these openings and there was no way for us to stay warm except by wearing heavy clothing or covering ourselves with blankets. Sometimes we woke up at night because the cold wind was blowing right into our faces.

We lived at least partially on the local economy. We purchased fresh vegetables daily from "Joe" who stopped his horse drawn cart in front of our house. His vegetables were huge: gigantic cauliflower one foot in diameter and equally large cabbages. The Navy doctor had issued instructions to wash all vegetables in Clorox because of the unsanitary conditions on the island. We did not do so because the vegetables no longer tasted like vegetables after being washed with Clorox. We bought meat from a butcher in a nearby village at sixty cents a pound regardless of the cut— liver, kidney, brain or filet mignon. We carried it away wrapped in newspapers.

Our maid, Delina, came to work six days a week for six hours each day. We paid her two pounds a week, or a little over five dollars, which was twice the going rate. The Maltese complained that we were spoiling the service personnel because we overpaid them by so much! All wage scales were this low. A worker in the British-owned dockyards earned six pounds a week, or less than twenty dollars. Delina was in her early twenties, but so restricted was her life that she had never even been in Valetta, although easily reachable by public bus from Lija where she lived. Delina was friendly and loved the children. Every day she washed the stone floors of the apartment on her knees. Most of the time Steven, who was two-years-old at the beginning and five at the end of our stay, was riding on her back as she scrubbed the floors. After we left Malta we remained in touch with her for many years.

An attractive feature of Balzan was a big park that surrounded the British governor's mansion. The park was open to the public. It contained almost all the trees still remaining on the island. In the summer we attended Shakespeare performances in this park. Spectators sat on plain wooden benches, which were little more than simple planks set up for this purpose. We dressed in shorts and tee-shirts, but the British came in formal wear, with the men in black tie and the women in evening dresses.

The Jewish community in Malta was made up of fifteen people, including women and children. They were three related families of British Jews who had settled in Malta after the war and opened businesses. For the High Holidays, they appealed to the British and American military services to send them enough Jewish men to hold religious observances. Ten adult men, a *minyan,* were required. Our Christian Navy chaplain asked me to attend the services. Years earlier there had been a thriving Jewish community in Malta, with a synagogue, a rabbi and a *mikveh,* the Jewish ritual bath. But this community had died out and all that was left was its abandoned cemetery.

Ruth and Steven, together with the children of other American families, went to a Montessori school run by nuns in a nearby convent. Every morning they dressed in their uniforms—cream colored shirt and tan pants or skirt, with a brown sweater in winter—and Ursel walked them the few blocks to school. They were well taken care of by the friendly nuns who respected that our children were Jewish and did not try to instruct them in the Catholic religion. The children learned a lot, and at times reversed the process, for instance at Passover when they "taught" the nuns about our Jewish customs. We celebrated *Hanukkah* and it was difficult to explain to my Navy colleagues that we did not celebrate Christmas. On Christmas Eve one of the enlisted men disguised himself as Santa Claus and visited all the American children on the island. We had no way to explain to him not to come to our house without offending him. We did not think our children were old enough for an explanation, and thought that Santa's visit would needlessly confuse them. We solved the dilemma by keeping a careful watch, and when we saw him in Balzan, we packed up the children and fled the house.

The United States maintained permanent bases in the Mediterranean to support anti-submarine warfare airplane squadrons which were rotated in from the States every six months. Twelve airplanes, nicknamed Neptunes, were stationed in Malta at all times. A Navy organization called Naval Aviation Engineering Service Unit, or NAESU for short, assigned an engineer to each facility to evaluate the performance of the planes' equipment, and to teach maintenance of the complex equipment to Navy technicians. I was a NAESU engineer.

I frequently flew on these Neptune planes, which had two propeller engines and two jets to assist in takeoffs. Once airborne, the planes could fly with the two jets alone. My first flight was just a few days after I arrived in Malta. I did not understand the separate functions of the propeller and jet engines. I was not even aware of the two jets. The eight-man crew knew I had never flown on a Neptune before, and shortly after take-off the crew chief pointed through the window and indicated that the right propeller engine had been feathered, that is, the engine had quit and the propeller placed in a safe position. He told me not to worry, we could go back on one engine. A few minutes later, with a worried expression he pointed at the left engine. It had also been feathered. Now, he said, we were in trouble. We would have to ditch in the sea. Who knew how that would come out? He requested me to put on my life jacket. Every crew member did the same. I was scared. I thought my life was over—so soon, so early. But the plane kept flying. I asked myself why weren't we losing altitude. The answer of course was the plane was flying on the jet engines—but I did not know it. Soon the feathered engines started to operate again. It had all been a practical joke staged for my benefit. I was not angry, and had no ill feelings. All I felt was relief. But the practical joke was a heavy one. In any event I was careful in choosing the pilots I flew with because some of them were young "hot shots" who broke the rules "for fun," and sometimes crashed as a consequence. I had no desire to become their victim.

For me, it was thrilling to simply step on an airplane and then fly off to various destinations in Europe and North Africa. I didn't need a ticket, most of the time I didn't even need a passport, just my military orders. I flew to London, Rome, Pisa, Barcelona, Nicosia in Cyprus and Rabat in Morocco. Sometimes during the flight, I sat in the cockpit next to the pilot, playing copilot. Flying over the Mediterranean at night, I was thrilled by the lights of the ships below and the stars above. It was sheer magic. I got to know Crete and Sardinia when I accompanied the squadrons on week-long maneuvers on the islands. At these times I lived on Navy ships, in tents and sometimes in luxurious BOQs, the bachelor officers quarters. One time I returned from Naples in a small four-seater plane, just the pilot and I. The pilot decided to take me sightseeing and we flew around the volcano Mount Etna in Sicily, round and round, inspecting the crater on top. Then we continued to Malta. The pilot had never landed in Malta. I was sitting next to him, and as he approached the field I suddenly realized he was headed to an abandoned airfield where the runway was blocked with barbed wire. I shouted a warning to him and at the last minute he lifted the airplane back up. A few minutes later we landed safely at the proper base.

Another time, in a small passenger plane, I landed on an aircraft carrier and then took off again after spending a day and a night on the huge ship. During my stay on board, I watched takeoffs and landings of the carrier's planes from the "vulture's nest." This was a lookout high on the ship. Carrier takeoffs and landings were dangerous, particularly the landings. A plane would come in at fairly high speed. Under its tail was a hook designed to snag a cable strung across the deck, and the cable would snap the plane to an abrupt stop. Sometimes the hook did not engage the cable and then the pilot would attempt to go around again and try once more. Occasionally the attempt failed and the plane crashed. Sailors would climb up to the vulture's nest to watch for such accidents. Fortunately, there were no accidents while I was in the vulture's nest. All this was exiting and added a dimension of adventure to my job. Leaving the carrier the plane dropped me off in Athens. I was on leave, and my destination was Israel. Before boarding the plane to Tel Aviv, I went to hear Isaac Stern in concert. When I got to the airport that evening, I discovered that Stern was also going to Israel, along with Leonard Bernstein, his wife Felicia, and some other musicians. They were going to play the inaugural concert in a new music hall in Tel Aviv. The plane had a problem and could not take off. It was Felicia's birthday. Isaac Stern took out his fiddle and entertained all of us as we waited for the plane to be serviced. He performed a remarkable twenty-minute improvisation on the theme of "Happy Birthday to You." Ever since, I have had a soft spot in my heart for Isaac Stern, and every time I have heard him play I remember that very special night at the airport in Athens. The plane was unable to take off that evening and we spent the rest of the night in a hotel provided by TWA. The next day I found myself sitting next to Leonard Bernstein. During the flight I tried to talk to him, but I could see that I distracted him from whatever he was thinking. His mind was elsewhere.

I did yet another kind of flying. In front of my office window was parked a utility airplane, a two engine DC-3, that was used the way we would have used a car if we had not been on an island. We flew in the DC-3 to attend meetings on the mainland, to bring in supplies and to take sick people to US military hospitals in Europe. In this plane, I went shopping in military Post Exchanges (PXs) in Naples and Tripoli, together with officers and enlisted men from our base. We bought American food and all sorts of other merchandise available in the PXs: cameras, clothing, pots and pans and even artificial flowers. The PXs were like miniature department stores. Soon our children learned that cottage cheese came from Naples and apple juice from Africa. Ruth and I flew to a US Air Force hospital in Germany in the DC-3 when she was loosing her hearing and nobody on the island—not our Navy doctor, not a local Maltese doctor, not the British medical specialist—could tell us what was wrong. They advised us that she would be permanently hard of hearing, if not deaf. A young American specialist at the hospital in Germany established the right diagnosis in a few minutes and provided a temporary treatment that restored her hearing for a while. After we returned home, Ruth was permanently cured.

This was the first time I had returned to Germany since I had left it as a child in 1939. As the plane lifted off from Malta, I felt anxious. I did not know what my reaction would be when I set foot again on German soil, after the events of those earlier years. In the end, I felt so inhibited when we arrived that I could not bring myself to speak a single word of German. It was evening when we got to the Ramstein Air Force Base and the cafeteria was already closed. Ruth and I walked to the small village outside the gate, I believe it was called Landstuhl, to have dinner. The waitress in the restaurant did not speak any English, and I could not bring myself to order in German. My five-year old daughter could not understand this. She pushed me with her elbow and said "Daddy, but you speak German!" How could I make her understand? I did not even try. It was not until several days later, on our way to Frankfurt to catch our return flight to Malta, that I overcame my inhibitions enough to speak German to the local people.

I almost lost my life on board the DC-3. One day I planned to fly to Naples to give a report on the progress of a project and told Ursel that I would be back in the late afternoon. I was sitting on the plane with the engines turning, ready for take-off, when a Naval officer with whom I had worked on the project got on to ask if he could go in my place because he wanted to do some shopping in the PX. I gave him my briefing papers and got off the plane. Since there were so few telephones in Malta, and none in our apartment, there was no way for me to tell Ursel that I had not gone on the trip. On its return flight, the plane crashed on takeoff, killing everyone in the front section, which was where I normally sat. Passengers in the back survived unhurt, except for my colleague who was not wearing a seatbelt and was thrown the length of the passenger cabin and broke his back. His injuries rendered him a paraplegic for life. When I came home that afternoon, I did not yet know about the accident. Five minutes later a neighbor came to tell us that the plane had crashed and that there had been injuries and fatalities. Had I not just arrived home, Ursel would have had to assume that I had been on that flight and been hurt or killed.

While in Malta we traveled widely and, for the first time, managed to save some money. In 1957, visiting Israel, we came under pressure from our relatives to stay and live there. Being in Israel made us feel nostalgic. Our relatives and friends were there, and we had come from an island where everybody was a stranger to us. Soon we would be going back to that island. My brother even arranged a job interview for me in the Israeli Ministry of Defense in Tel Aviv. He advised them that I would be in Israel for only a few days. When we got to the ministry, nobody was available to speak to us and we were told to return some other day. I did not return, but six months later I got a letter in Malta, asking me to present myself for an interview the following day—but of course the date had long since passed! In any event, by this time the emotions we had experienced on that first visit to Israel had passed, and we were no longer thinking of relocating there.

When we arrived in Malta we had practically no money, and we were living hand-to-mouth. By the time we left, we had saved enough to finance my future studies at the university. I was fortunate, because this meant I wouldn't have to work while pursuing my studies. Malta was considered a hardship post and I received extra pay. In addition to my salary, I also received a daily living allowance for being away from home; home being considered Rochester. Under the prevailing tax law, we were not required to pay any income taxes, and life on Malta was so cheap that we could not spend all the money we earned even if we had wanted to. It was the only time in our lives that we felt what it must be like to be wealthy!

In 1959 the American base on Malta was to be moved to Catania in Sicily. We could have extended our assignment for another year, but we did not want to start over again in yet another country. In any case, we felt it was time to come home. Under an agreement with the Navy, those of us who had volunteered for overseas assignments were allowed to choose our next place of work in any one of a number of cities on either coast. We liked Washington, and thought it provided great proximity to the amenities of New York and other east coast cities. I requested a headquarters assignment in Washington, and Bethesda became our new home. We liked it so much we never left!

The Rest of the Story

The time has come to conclude this story. After we returned in August 1959, we found a spacious four bedroom apartment. Since we had departed Chile ten years earlier, we had moved—country to country, city to city—seven times. It was time to settle down and end this gypsy life. The children started going to school, and we became acquainted with our new neighbors. Many of them, both Americans and foreigners, were scientists at the National Institutes of Health (NIH), which was across the fence from where we lived. Proper medical treatment soon cured Ruth of her hearing problem. On August 3, 1960, our second son and last child, Daniel, was born.

I quit NAESU in 1962 when its headquarters were moved to Philadelphia. We did not want to move again. I found a new job in bioengineering to work on the development of a computer system that analyzed cardiograms and determined heart diseases automatically. Quitting NAESU also meant quitting

Stromberg-Carlson, which had become part of a much larger company called General Dynamics.

On the weekend between jobs we celebrated the birthday of Ursel and Ruth. On that same weekend, Ursel and I were in a bad car accident in which both of us were injured—Ursel much worse than me. We were on our way to the theater to see a performance of a Shakespeare play and to join a couple we had recently met. A few blocks from our house, a sixteen-year-old boy driving a Cadillac ran a red light at high speed and hit our Volkswagen broadside. We never arrived at the theater and landed in the nearest hospital instead.

Due to the fact that I was between jobs for those two days, we were without any insurance when the accident occurred. The previous policy had lapsed when I resigned from Stromberg-Carlson, and the new policy would not become effective until the following Monday when I was scheduled to start my new job. On that Monday morning I called my former supervisor from the hospital and told him about our accident. He showed an admirable understanding for our situation and offered to put me back on the payroll, since he had not yet turned in my resignation papers to the personnel department. That way I remained an employee, retaining both my salary and my insurance. I was grateful to him. I remained on the payroll for three weeks until I started my new job. The previous insurance remained in force and covered most of the enormous medical expenses that were required to provide Ursel the care she needed.

I was released from the hospital after a couple of days, but Ursel remained for six weeks. Her pelvis had fractured in multiple places, and she had broken ribs and a fractured nose, as well as many contusions. Her treatment was extremely painful. Before I left the hospital, her doctors told me that she would never walk again. She came home on a walker and started exercising with great energy and willpower. Ultimately, she proved the doctors wrong. Within a few months she was able to walk normally. While we both were in the hospital, an Israeli family, neighbors we had just met, took charge of our children. We became such close friends that we considered each other to be family.

I had become uneasy about my lack of a university degree. Private industry now insisted on such a degree when they hired engineers. Beyond that, I felt inferior to other engineers with formal degrees. I had undertaken my institute studies in the 1950s as an expedient to finish quickly so that we could leave for Israel as soon as possible. Of course, we never left, and it was now time to rectify the consequences of that earlier decision. I was accepted for graduate studies at several universities, including George Washington University in Washington, DC. Due to the medical and legal consequences of the accident, we could not move away. Although I seriously considered other opportunities, George Washington was the only feasible choice. With our savings from Malta, the help of a NASA fellowship, and one year as a graduate teaching assistant, we had enough resources for me to go to school full time. In 1964, I earned my Master of Science degree in Engineering. It was a proud and happy moment for me, the fulfillment of a dream that I had held dating back to my teenage years in Chile and even earlier. After defending my thesis and being told by my thesis master that I had passed, "the best ever," I left by train to join Ursel and the kids at a lakeside resort near New York City where they were vacationing. During the hours it took me to get there, I could hardly contain my joy. It was a great day.

I continued to study for my doctorate the following year, but we needed a steady income for the family. While the Master's degree was essential, the doctorate was gravy. I did not envision an academic career for myself. Rather, I wanted to be a practicing engineer. For that, a Ph.D. was not essential. I left the university to look for work.

I received an offer from Bell Laboratories to perform systems analysis for Apollo, the first manned mission to the moon. I took the job, but I wanted to be closer to the action—I wanted to work for NASA. After one year at Bell, I was offered a position at NASA's Goddard Space Flight Center in Greenbelt, Maryland, which I accepted happily. I remained at NASA for twenty-two years. During my last years there I managed the development of an international search and rescue system that used satellites to locate aircraft and ships in distress. The timely rescues made possible by this system saved the lives of many accident victims who otherwise would have been lost. Ultimately, the system proved so successful that it was implemented worldwide. One day I received a telephone call from the University of Chile, which had decided to develop a ground station for this system as a research project. The Chilean project team leader wanted me to assist them. I was happy to respond to their needs. I retained strong emotional ties to the country and felt that by giving them the help they needed I was able to pay back in small measure the large debt I owed Chile for having saved my life decades earlier.

I had now come full circle in my career: from helping to destroy submarines and their crews I was now helping to save the lives of thousands of people who would have perished without that help. When I retired from NASA in 1988, I felt that I could not have asked for a more satisfying conclusion to my career.

It was not, however, the end of my professional life. I worked for a few more years for private industry. When I was sixty-six, I experienced what many others had experienced earlier in life but I had been spared: I was laid off. The company I worked for closed its doors and fired all of its 850 employees on the same day. I was almost happy. I had wanted to retire but had procrastinated making the decision. Now the decision had been made for me.

Fifty years had passed since I first went to work. It was time to stop. For a long time, I had planned to study subjects I had neglected earlier in life. I went back to my alma mater to take courses unrelated to engineering: literature and philosophy. At the same time, I continued to work occasionally on the search and rescue project, assisting the government agency in charge, no longer NASA, to implement the system in Latin America. The combination of my knowledge of Spanish and my understanding of the system were ideal for this task. It was work I enjoyed. I met with many Latin Americans who were grateful not only for my technical help, but also that I provided it in Spanish. As part of this work, I attended meetings in Latin American countries several times a year. These activities turned out to be both a professional and cultural enrichment for my post-retirement years.

In the 1960s, Ursel began thinking about completing her own education and beginning a second career. Until then, she had been absorbed by taking care of the household and our children. She thought it was time to broaden her horizons, but did not know what to choose as a profession. Perhaps she could make use of her knowledge of languages to become an interpreter, or maybe a teacher. A chance course at a junior college provided the answer. The college required a science course and she chose zoology solely for convenience; it was the only course that fit into her daily schedule. But with this course she had found her destiny, her calling. The course work appealed to her and she realized that she wanted to pursue life sciences as a profession. She enrolled at the University of Maryland to study microbiology, and in 1980 obtained her Master of Science degree. At age fifty-two, she was ready to start her career as a research scientist. She was hired by the Cancer Institute of the National Institutes of Health to do cancer research. She liked her work, was very successful, published numerous papers and she continues to have a fulfilling career.

In 1965 we bought a house in Bethesda not far from the apartment where we had been living. It was large enough for each child to have a separate bedroom, and it had a porch, a patio and a backyard full of trees. Our arrival in this new home meant we had put an end to our wandering gypsy life. One of our goals was to provide a stable environment for the children to grow up, where they could form lasting friendships and feel that they had a permanent home. By buying a house close to where we had lived previously, we were able to accomplish that goal.

As the children grew up, each made her or his own way in life after completing their university studies. Ruth got married under the trees in our backyard in 1975. She and her husband, Phil Shapiro, have three daughters: Elisa, Laura and Tamara who now are nineteen, seventeen and fifteen, respectively. Ruth made the choice of bringing up her children before starting to work outside the home. Steven chose marketing as his career. He married Nancy Cascella, in 1993. A boy, Robbie (Robert), was born on Independence Day 1994. Steven had been born on Chile's Independence Day, the *Dieciocho* (September 18th). Their second son, James, was born three years later in June 1997. Daniel is a mathematician. He followed in his mother's footsteps, and is now doing bio-mathematical research at the Cancer Institute of NIH.

We have lived in Bethesda for more than thirty-eight years, much longer than anywhere else. During these years we acquired many new friends, and kept in touch with old friends living in Israel, Chile and Germany through correspondence and occasional visits. I discovered surviving classmates from Königsberg living here in the US, in Israel, Germany and Switzerland and we have become friends. We developed a close relationship with Ursel's family in Chile: a cousin, her three daughters and their husbands and children. We found in them a warm and loving family that we had neglected for many years. Our family relationship became so close that when Ivonne, the oldest daughter, got married in 1988, she invited me to come to Chile to give her away at her wedding because her father had died many years earlier. We traveled to Santiago and I was happy and proud of the honor.

Over the years, we have had many visitors. My mother came, our brothers with their wives and children and friends and relatives from Chile and Israel. My former classmate and our later friend, Judith Wolff, with whom I had been in love with at age eight, visited often from Switzerland. She died unexpectedly in 1995 and we missed her greatly.

After my first trip from Malta in 1958 to take Ruth to the US Air Force hospital, I have returned to Germany many times, at first professionally as a NASA engineer and later as a tourist. I have overcome the inhibitions I felt on the earlier trip but my ambivalent feelings have remained. In some ways I feel at home in Germany. My native language, my cultural heritage are German. But at the same time what Germany did to me, to my friends and family, to my whole people, weighs heavily on my mind every time I set foot in Germany. I cannot forget. When I first visited Berlin in 1970 and went to the wall which at that time separated the East and West sectors of the city, I saw the many crosses erected in front of the wall to commemorate those who had tried to cross to the West and had been shot dead in the attempt by East German guards who had caught them. Germans had told me of their families living on the other side, whom they could not ever visit. The formerly brilliant city, one of the most brilliant in Europe, was destroyed, divided and desolate. When I stood on top of the wall and looked across to the East, my first reaction to all that was "what a tragedy." But in a flash, in a split second reaction, my second thought was "but it serves them right." That reaction to Germany has never left me. I feel it every time I visit.

Several times we visited our family and friends in Israel. On our visits we have stayed in my brother's *kibbutz*, where also my mother lived until her death in 1974, or the *kibbutz* where Ursel's brother lived before he and his family left it and moved away to town. This provided us with the opportunity to observe close up what our life would have been like if we had not chosen to abandon the Movement before we left Chile. Life in the *kibbutz* has changed over the years. Living standards have greatly increased and the economy is no longer based on agriculture. Instead, each *kibbutz* now derives most of its income from industrial enterprises, some successful, others less so. These enterprises employ many workers and even managers from the outside, who are not members of the *kibbutz*. Some *kibbutzim* are on the verge of bankruptcy and depend on subsidies from wealthier *kibbutzim* to continue their existence. Ideology no longer rules life. Individual members own much private property. Children live with their parents and no longer in separate children's houses. Members are paid for their work and in turn pay for their food and other necessities. Some *kibbutzim* are considering differential pay depending on the work each member performs instead providing equal pay to all as is the case now. All these changes would have been inconceivable in past times. Many children, more than fifty percent, do not return to the *kibbutz* after their obligatory army service but instead move to town with its greater opportunities. This process of greater individualization is dynamic and continuing. Some members predict the demise of the *kibbutz* as an organization, bringing an end to one of the great social experiments in collective living in this century.

I do not regret our decision not to settle on a *kibbutz*. Fewer of our relatives now reside there: my brother died in 1990 before his sixty-fifth birthday, and two of his three children left the *kibbutz*. Ursel's brother and family abandoned *kibbutz* life many years ago in favor of the city.

Our lives developed in ways beyond anything we could have expected when we moved here. From a small town environment, Washington has grown into an international cultural center. In ever increasing abundance, it offers us operas and concerts, theater and world class museum exhibitions. We do not limit our cultural activities to Washington. We have traveled as close as Baltimore and as far away as San Francisco and Seattle for special events, and we have paid many a visit to New York. The more recent presence of our family in New York adds an additional incentive to these visits.

We also visited Europe, South America, Israel and Egypt. Although I frequently traveled alone on NASA business, Ursel and I have taken many trips together. Ever since I was a teenager, I dreamed of seeing Machu Picchu in Peru and of exploring Egypt. Those dreams became a reality when we made extended visits to both places in the 1980s. We took long hikes in Germany together with two rediscovered classmates from my childhood, Michael Wieck and Judith, both of whom I have mentioned earlier in this account. We also took extended trips to many other countries in Europe. Everywhere we have traveled we have soaked up the atmosphere, the culture, the food, nature and the landscapes, and every one of these trips has contributed to the enrichment of our lives.

Reflections

In July 1997, twelve surviving students of the Königsberg Jewish School and their spouses met in New Jersey for a reunion. Three others were invited but could not attend. Seventy students out of 180 were still in Königsberg when the deportations began. All seventy were murdered as were some students who had left Königsberg for other cities in Germany. Of those who were sent to Holland with children's transports, some were caught by the Germans after they invaded Holland and were also murdered, but others escaped and were hidden by Dutch families for the duration of the war. There is no reliable estimate of their number. Our reunion of survivors was a poignant occasion. A minute of silence before dinner during the first night commemorated our schoolmates and teachers who had not survived. Later we each retold the stories of our escapes and what had happened to us since. We looked at pictures of children from the school and identified our special friends among them. All of us had saved those pictures as treasured mementos. None of the survivors at the reunion were my classmates. No matter. What bound us together were our memories of the school, its students and teachers. Just talking about them was a catharsis. We shared feelings and thoughts that we had kept bottled up within us for decades. We had been able to defy the Nazi hordes that wanted to destroy us—many of whom were later themselves destroyed in the war. That all by itself provided a note of triumph, at least to me.

In December of the same year, I met three other surviving schoolmates in Israel. One of them had escaped the Nazis in Holland and had been hidden by a Catholic family at great peril to themselves. She had been my classmate and playmate, and for many years, decades, I had thought her dead and mourned her. My feelings in meeting these three women were similar to what I felt at our survivor's reunion six months earlier.

I reflected on how close I had come to sharing the fate of those who were deported in the cattle cars and shot in Riga—or wherever they met their end. How miraculous had been my escape! I shudder to think about the last moments of those who were not so lucky: my relatives, my friends, my teachers, my fellow students and all the others who were on those horrible trains. My imagination freezes at the various sites of their executions—the moment before each received a fatal bullet or was shoved into the gas chambers at the death camps. I cannot comprehend those horror-filled moments, and find myself incapable of comprehending the incomprehensible.

I cannot help but be thankful for the life I have lived: my youth as a Jewish child in Nazi Germany and the poverty and lack of education I experienced in Chile did not offer the promise of a rosy future. For a long while I thought life on a *kibbutz* would offer a way out, but it would have lead to a restrictive life that was subject to the will of others. I did not want that. It was far better to struggle and find a different solution. A spirit of determination and adventure led Ursel and me on our lifelong journey. Our determination to pursue our lives in our own way carried the day. We left Chile and the prospects offered by the Movement behind, and chose to create a new way for ourselves in a new land. Fortunately, our effort has been crowned by success. I think of success as having a loving family that includes children and grandchildren, college education that led to satisfying professions for both of us, new and old friendships, the opportunity to pursue our cultural interests and finally the opportunity to travel to all those places in the world that held a special interest for us.

Again and again I come back to the thought that none of this could have come about without the miracle that happened in Königsberg in 1939 that allowed my family and me to escape from Germany. The fact that I was not shoved into one of those cattle cars and shot at the end of the ride is a miracle for which I am eternally grateful.

My story comes to a happy end, and finds Ursel and me still living in our home in Bethesda, grateful for each other, and grateful for the wonderful family we share. From now on it is up our children and grandchildren to carry the story forward into the future.

Fred Flatow
Bethesda, Maryland, January 1998

Glossary

German

Bademeister	swimming pool manager
CV	Abbreviated name of Jewish German organization favoring assimilation
Deutschland	Germany: "Deutschland, Deutschland" was the beginning of the German anthem at that time
Dom	Cathedral
Frau	Mrs.
Fräulein	Miss
Führer	Leader, generally refers to Hitler
Götterdämmerung	Twilight of the Gods, opera by Richard Wagner
Gymnasium	German high school
Grüne Brücke	Green Bridge
Hauptbahnhof	main railway station
Heimat, Heimatland	homeland
Herr	Mister
Jude, Juden	Jew, Jews
Judenhäuser	Jews' houses. After 1939, the Nazis started to concentrate Jews in such houses
Juden nicht erwünscht	signs in Nazi Germany forbidding entry of Jews to shops, theaters, etc.
Kaffee und Kuchen	coffee and cake
Kaiserstrasse	Street of the Emperors, where I lived in Königsberg
Kinderheim	children's vacation home
Kennkarte	identity card
Krämer Brücke	Tradesmen's Bridge
Kristallnacht	Crystal Night, German Pogrom on the 9th and 10th of November, 1938
Lied	song
Lift	large container used to transport household goods
Nordbahnhof	Northern Railway Station
N.S.D.A.P.	abbreviation for German Nazi party
Onkel	uncle
ORFA	abbreviation for Ostpreussische Regenmäntelfabrik, my parent's factory
Riesengebirge	Mountains of the Giants, a mountain range near the Czech border

SA	Nazi Storm Troopers
Stürmer	one who storms, name of an anti-Semitic newspaper in Nazi Germany
Tante	aunt
Valhalla	dwelling of the Gods in Wagner's opera cycle "The Ring of the Nibelung"
Zeitung	newspaper, journal

Hebrew/Yiddish

aliyah	"to go up," applied to migration to Israel
Bar Mitzvah	religious initiation ceremony of a Jewish boy at age thirteen
bima	pulpit in a synagogue
challah	ceremonial twisted white bread for the Sabbath and other holidays
chasan	cantor
Chevra Kadisha	burial society
hachsharah	preparatory farm for life on a *kibbutz*
Haftorah	readings from the Prophets
Haggada	prayer book for the Passover eve celebration
Hanukkah	Holiday lasting eight days, celebrated in December
Hashomer Hatzaïr	Young Guardian, worldwide Zionist youth organization
horrah	Israeli folk dance
Kaddish	prayer for the dead
kibbutz, kibbutzim	collective farm(s) in Israel
Kiddush	prayer recited on the eve of the Sabbath and other holidays
Kidma	Zionist youth organization in Chile
kvutzah	community, designation applied to age related small groups in the *Kidma*
Maccabi	Jewish sports organization
MAPAM	United Workers Party, labor party in Israel
matzah	unleavened bread eaten during Passover
mikveh	Jewish ritual bath
minyan	a minimum of ten adult males required for communal prayer

Rosh Hashanah	Jewish New Year
Seder	Order, name given to the celebration of the first two evenings of Passover
Shalshelet	Chain, here a name of a kvutzah in the *Kidma*
shammes	sexton
Smah Yisrael	"Hear, Oh Israel," principal Jewish prayer
shul	prayer room, synagogue
Torah	five Books of Moses, handwritten on a parchment scroll
Yom Kippur	Day of Atonement, celebrated ten days after Rosh Hashanah

Spanish

cazuela	Chilean vegetable and meat soup
cerro	hill
CISROCO	abbreviation for Israelite Aid Committee
conventillo	tenement house
cordillera	mountain range
cuecas, tonadas	Chilean folk dance and folk music
Dieciocho	eighteen, applied to the 18th of September, Chile's Independence Day
humanidades	Chilean high school
M.N.S.	abbreviation for Chile's Nazi party
mozo	servant
pensión	boarding house
preparatorias	Chilean grade school
Puro Chile	"Pure Chile," the beginning of the Chilean anthem
roto chileno	"broken Chilean," euphemism for member of the poorest class
Señor	Mister
serrucho	Chilean expression for a transit inspector
taller	repair or work shop
Teatro Municipal	Municipal Theater, Santiago's opera house and concert hall